# Be Rich with Specunomics

Kushal Thaker

PAGE PUBLISHING, INC.
Conneaut Lake, PA

First originally published by Page Publishing 2021

ISBN 978-1-6624-6511-6 (pbk)
ISBN 978-1-6624-6512-3 (digital)

Printed in the United States of America

# Contents

# Acknowledgments

This first book of mine would not have been possible without the help of these important persons:

*Ritu Shah*, who deserves the most credit for all her hard work in bringing this book to life;

*Priya Parekh*, my sweet sister who assisted me to pen down my thoughts;

*Amit Khatri*, my associate, for his invaluable support;

and finally, the person who inspired me to write this book, *Nimesh Rathod*, the business acumen coach and friend.

# Origin

The Latin word *speculatur*, past participle of *speculari*, means "to watch over, explore, *reconnoitre*" (word used in military campaigns—to make an observation through exploration).

In the late fourteenth century, it was "intelligent contemplation, the act of looking," from Old French *Speculacion*, which means "close observation, rapt attention."

And soon, the word *speculan* meant "pursuit of the truth by means of thinking" in the mid fifteenth century.

A disparaging sense of "mere conjecture" is recorded from the 1570s.

In 1774 came the meaning we understand clearly today, "buying and selling in search of profit from rise and fall of market value."

And so market value is of any asset.

If so, what we are doing as speculators is nothing short of a precision-based speculation on an asset class to make profit from it, given a predetermined time horizon.

A speculator is a person who gathers intelligence through all the data collected or observed and comes to a conclusion as to the strategy to be designed and structured toward the approach of taking positions on the asset class to make profits.

Mind well the horizon of the position varies from speculator to speculator, but all of them can be right depending on their individual time horizon.

Every human is a speculator and speculates on something or the other every day in their life.

An office goer speculates as to which route to take to reach his destination faster, or a homemaker speculates with a new cooking dish learned and how to adjust the taste to her family's liking.

A student speculates about certain questions that can be left as options in the coming exams.

A surgeon speculates on a tricky or risky surgery that is likely to happen.

A civil engineer speculates, through intense study of the topography of city structures in existence, to build a metro through it.

And so on...

Hence all of us collect and study intensely a lot of parameters that are thrown to us as data, and from all the incomplete data collected, we study them to arrive at a conclusion for a beneficial result.

# Why This Book

The purpose of this book is to bring the world of speculation to all and to say that it is being practiced since the human race is there. All of us have the potential of a speculator, and we need to harness it to our advantage because an individual speculates always in an unknowing manner.

But once this unknowing attribute of behavior can be made known to oneself, the mind starts getting cultivated in the direction needed to go.

Here, I bring out the psyche or the mindset needed to take decisions from all the uncertainties and chaos around us. The situation can unravel in any form, and we have to make it profitable.

I consider meditation and speculation in close proximity as in both; control of the mind in a disciplined and focused manner brings absolute positive results.

Though this book is to bring the world of investments, trading, and speculation closer to you, I want to see every person distanced from the world of finance and markets to pick this copy and develop the ability to profit from investments.

People from finance world will be able to understand the markets and its implications on daily life much better than the non-market-oriented.

I am writing this book with the simplest of language for all to understand. I have not used any complicated and technical jargons commonly used in the financial world.

For me, the success of this book is when

1.  a college graduate, after reading this book, decides to go independent in the markets and use it as a base to make money for his own living and beyond;
2.  when a housewife/homemaker, even if he/she does not become an investment trader in the market, can develop the ability to think, understand the movement of commodities used in daily life, and make future budgeting forecast of the family/personal expenses; or
3.  a businessman/industrialist who needs to integrate backward and forward his business operations where commodities play the role as either a raw material or a finished good.

# Chapter 1

## Investment and Speculation Confusion

Dictionary.com says to put capital in order to gain profitable returns.

As per *Merriam-Webster*, it is "the outlay of money usually for income or profit."

As per *Oxford Dictionary*, it is "an act of devoting time, effort or energy to a particular undertaking with expectation of a worthwhile result."

Now seeing and reading the above definitions and comparing it with the meaning of speculation written earlier, both terms are processes to achieve the same end, which is "make money, make profits, and create wealth."

The stalwarts of the field of finance still distinguish between the two by saying and stating various times that investment is good and speculation is not so good.

The term *investment*, when used, brings us a sense of clarity or at least commitment. This is how it has been perceived or ingrained in the minds of the people.

And the term *speculation* suggests uncertainty, a guess, or even a gamble.

(The distinction between speculation and gamble shall be discussed in the following pages.)

Speculation is commonly used to describe leveraged transactions or decisions purely of direction and momentum of prices, and hence, speculation has often been denied by many of the respected members of the society.

And here I say very strongly that the thinking given above is a far shout from their original meaning.

Some people argue that the time horizon is a criterion distinguishing the two, and I say NEVER.

Speculation too can have a large time horizon as speculators are using valuations to arrive at decisions for buying or selling an asset.

When we say a person has to "cut the coat" as per his size or a person must know his own limitations, such quotes are applicable to both, the so-called players or traders in the market. Hence, I consider the two terms as same.

Many people use the word *speculation* to risky investments, and the word *risky* is usually used when the investment is made in assets of low quality or uncertain outlook.

But what is *high quality* and *safe investment* then?

Have we not seen high-quality and safe investment stocks collapse and bite the dust? Or you could have held on to an asset for years thinking it was the safest and still wound up making negligible returns or notional losses.

So this position taken that was done a few years ago which was perceived as an investment and now is reduced to dust, as when unanticipated risks come and tend to result in losses, should this be called speculative or investment loss?

And here I quote John Maynard Keynes, "A speculator runs the risk of which he is aware and an investor is one who runs the risk of which he is unaware."

We are all speculators after all. We know our risk parameters, and we know our achievable gains.

And when the risk parameters are not studied, that is what makes a gambler. Now I am bringing out the distinction between a speculator and a gambler.

A speculator is professional, honorable, intellectual, serious, analytical, calm, selective, and focused.

Whereas a gambler is distracted, moody, impulsive, desperate, and superstitious.

The gambler usually enters a trade or casino to place a bet on races and on slot machines without understanding the odds against them, and he goes all out in taking positions that can also be the road to ruin.

In contrast, a speculator knows his risk/reward criteria distinctly and will act on it.

The Indians in particular distinguish between the two words, *satta* and *jugar*, clearly. *Satta* is speculation, and *jugar* is gambling. People use both the words carelessly to bring speculation a bad meaning.

***So I say satta is good; speculation is good.***

# Chapter 2

## Traders Are Not Born, They Are Made

The title of this chapter should give relief to the minds of all that anyone who follows certain amount of discipline and average intelligence in life can become one. We shall go in depth into this in the analytical part of this book.

Trading is a skill-based activity in which we make decisions under conditions of uncertainty and risk. We can have uncertainty without risk, but it is impossible to have risk without uncertainty.

Let me come out with a real-life experiment.

A neuroscientist led by the institute of Prof. Ann Graybiel found that untrained monkeys performing a simple visual scanning task gradually developed efficient patterns that allowed them to minimize the time it took to receive their reward.

The findings not only revealed how the brain forms habits but also shed light on neurological disorders changed to habit formation results in highly repetitive behavior, such as Tourette's syndrome, obsessive compulsive disorder, and schizophrenia.

In the same way, the process of trading, from scanning the markets (like we have used the term *reconnoitre* before on page 1) for a setup to closing the position, consists of a sequence of tasks. Over time, we create habits by combining these tasks together in a process.

So perhaps good traders aren't born but, rather, made. Traders are made by the habits they form. It takes, on average, twenty-one days to join a habit and ninety days to form a lifestyle.

Certain characteristic traits, namely conscientiousness with two of its facets, self-efficiency and self-discipline, lend themselves nicely to forming good habits, as opposed to the traits such as neuroticism that can lead to bad habits. It is therefore important to know what characteristic or trait one brings to the forefront.

If you have been in the markets for a while and find yourself unsuccessful, the culprit may be the habits and the biases you have formed early in your trading. Human brains have difficult time in distinguishing between good and bad habits. The good news is that bad habits can be changed into good habits through interrupting the habit cycle and changing the routine. Interrupting this cycle is easier than it sounds and well worth the effort as longevity in the markets as a successful speculator is the reward.

## Speculation Helps Human Progress

Speculation in all its forms is what drives human progress. Michael Biggers's essay on the desire to speculate leaves a distinct message. It is said that the desire to speculate is very strong in the people. Reference is not merely to stock speculations but to the word in its broadest sense. Every new undertaking is a speculation.

An inventor speculates on what he is going to invent, and often, such speculations result in losses because many inventors or would-be inventors never accomplish very much. They spend their money, time, and efforts and probably live in poverty, and then if the invention is not profitable, they lose all.

It is the same thing with every new business. It is purely a speculation.

A student speculates as to what career he wants to take seeing the reward he is likely to get in coming years.

Now here comes a point that is greatly misunderstood by ignorant politicians, journalists, and everyday people, they refer to speculators as wicked people who somehow conspire to drive prices of assets higher or plunge them lower.

Any human activity that requires foresight and planning and the assumption of risk of money and labor is a form of speculation.

VCs (venture capitalists) speculate with their partner's capital when they back a new technology firm or a startup that makes EVs (electric vehicles).

Traders may speculate with their own money (and emotional capital) that some catalysts will serve to send prices of a share or a commodity higher or lower in the days or months ahead.

In other words, we speculate when we imagine something new or create some new business or invention or vote with our money on future outcomes.

As Bermard Banich says, the essence of speculation is to look out toward a great distance and try to observe the future developments.

# Chapter 3

## Are You a Bull or a Bear?

Individuals who have come in my contact always ask whether I am a bull or a bear on the market or the economy. My response often irritates them when I say, "I am neither—I am just an opportunist."

By this, I mean that I go out of my way to avoid placing myself into a neat and tidy category that can influence my analysis of the markets and the commodities/stocks I trade. Although I am far from perfect and sometimes let my opinions cloud my judgment (I am also a human after all), I do really try to do everything I can to look for opportunities on both sides of the market.

Many investors and traders try to fit themselves based on their opinions or of others whom they have come to respect or sometimes receive. Even worse, those views are frequently tainted by how the portfolio is currently positioned (every person wants to be right, after all), which can turn out to be dangerous as well as quite unprofitable.

I come across several traders who are struggling at some point because they have very strong views about the market, and actually, the market is completely against them. I never let such views cloud my own analysis and trading. I am fairly confident there would come a time when their views will be proven correct, but in this business, timing is everything. Opinions do not pay my bills—only profitable trades do!

Remember, in this business, it isn't about who is right or wrong. Instead, it is all about who can make money and take advantage of the most opportunities in the present. Opinions are terrific things, but in most cases, you would be wise to set them aside and trade the market you see rather than the market you think you should or want to see.

# Chapter 4

## Specunomics and Specumatics

The two words, *Specunomics* and *Specumatics*, are coined by me.

Specunomics simply means that speculation can be done successfully and profitably by following the simple principles of economics. By simple principles, I mean

- production/supply,
- consumption/demand,
- government policies,
- trade barriers,
- changes in consumption patterns,
- substitution effect during the price elasticity/inelasticity phase, and
- cost escalations due to capital/labor.

Specumatics—A simple comparison for the above over designated time frames can result in a trend, and the calculations of that for analysis is just mathematics that helps us to speculate, and hence I call it specumatics.

One of the most mystifying parts of speculation is the notion that the biggest opportunities come before a signal, and that is why knowing the fundamentals and visualizing the future is very important.

Now let's understand economics in a simple manner, and the parameters we always need to keep in mind to make ourselves analytical.

Economics—A branch of knowledge concerned with the production, distribution, and consumption of goods and services. In other words, it can also be said that "transfer of wealth" is happening.

It is the field or study that begins with the premise that any resource or asset class is scarce, and it becomes necessary to choose between competing alternatives—that eventually affects all patterns of demand and supply of the influenced asset, thus altering the production process, which is a reflection of the altered consumption process resulting in major shift of trends, and all the tradeoffs that are created become an economic cycle.

And these cycles are always in existence in some phase, and that when rightly analyzed is the opportunity cost that has to be maximized to generate riches and wealth.

# Chapter 5

# The Rise and Fall of Asset Classes

Though historically there were three main asset classes, equities (stocks), fixed income (bonds), and cash equivalent or money instruments. And in current times it even includes real estate, commodities, futures, other financial derivatives, and even cryptocurrencies.

Asset classes have their cycle of rise and falls. Every country follows different economic policies depending on the asset class they possess, and on its basis, they regulate their trades with other countries. If correct policies aren't framed as per the need of the hour, then that country's economy and its strong owned asset face the consequences.

Example of asset classes are as follows:

## Commodities

Every country's main source of survival and strength is their abundance of natural resources. The economy of the country depends on this and also the rise and fall of its economy. Commodities drive the country and not the other way round as what many theorists say.

Commodity prices during recessions and slowdown prices are adjusted for inflation and are shown in real terms.

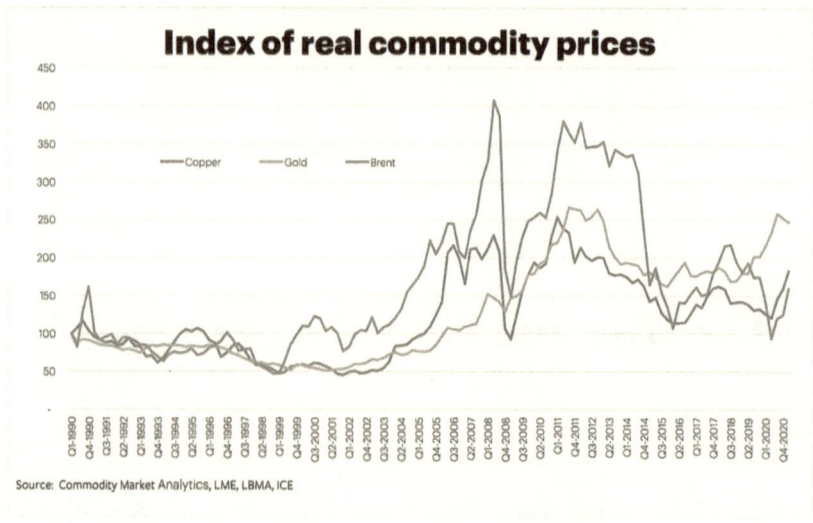

(Source: https://cygnetsearch.com)

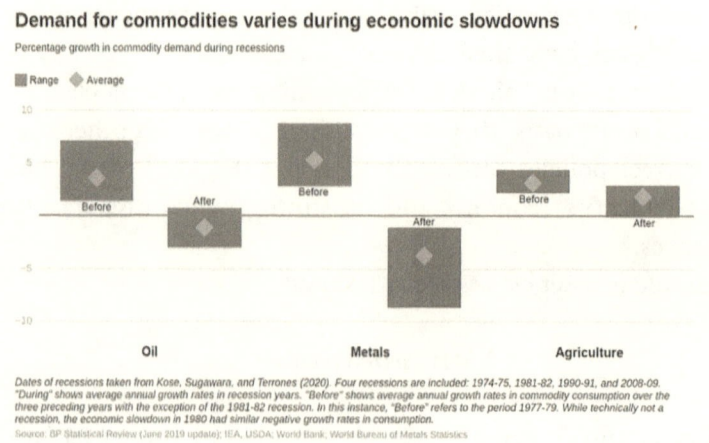

(Source: www.worldbank.org)

# Inflated Commodity Prices Precedes Recessions and Slowdowns

Before the recession of 1980s and 1990s, parabolic price movement in copper, gold, and crude oil were seen, though every commodity has their own independent cycles (explained in the later chapter).

Copper Price Movement in the Commodity Cycle

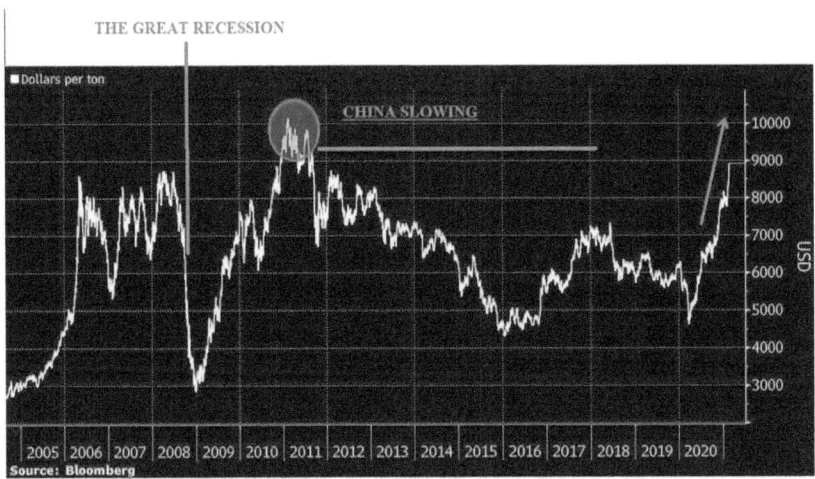

Below is the movement of CRB index that carries weight of nineteen components, which portrays a clear picture.

## The Components of the CRB Index and Commodity Super Cycle

The CRB index is calculated using the arithmetic average of commodity futures prices with monthly rebalancing. The index consists of nineteen commodities: aluminum, cocoa, coffee, copper, corn, cotton, crude oil, gold, heating oil, lean hogs, live cattle, natural gas, nickel, orange juice, RBOB gasoline, silver, soybeans, sugar, and wheat. Those commodities are sorted into four groups with different weightings: energy—39%, agriculture—41%, precious metals—7%, base/industrial metals—13%.

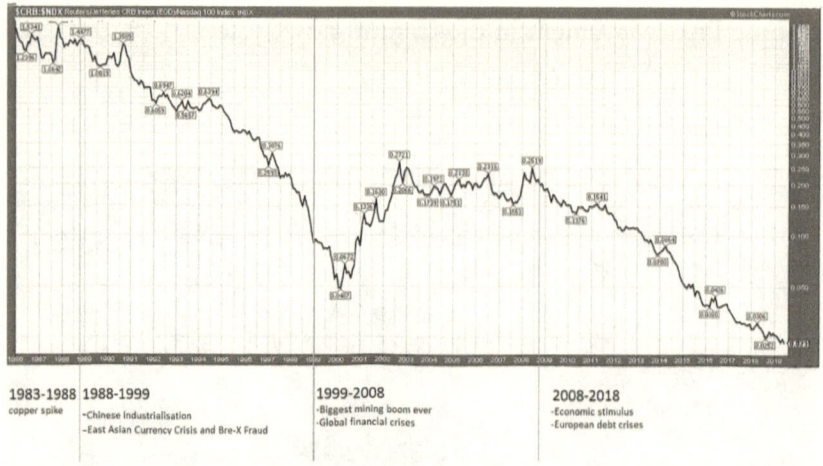

| 1983-1988 | 1988-1999 | 1999-2008 | 2008-2018 |
| --- | --- | --- | --- |
| copper spike | -Chinese Industrialisation<br>-East Asian Currency Crisis and Bre-X Fraud | -Biggest mining boom ever<br>-Global financial crises | -Economic stimulus<br>-European debt crises |

The commodity super cycle started in 2000s. The boom was largely fueled by roaring demand for emerging economies like the BRICS nations, especially China since the 1990s, which was gobbling up all the commodities from oil to metals to food to satisfy its voracious population's demand. The subprime crisis, the fall of the Lehman Brothers, went down in history from where started the financial crisis that lasted for two years. Since 2010, the cycle again saw an upswing, which finally resulted in crude oil prices breaching $100 and going as high as $145 till the Arab Spring hit the markets. The Saudis also tried to throw America out of oil market by flooding the market with excess crude oil supply, which eventually backfired on its own economy.

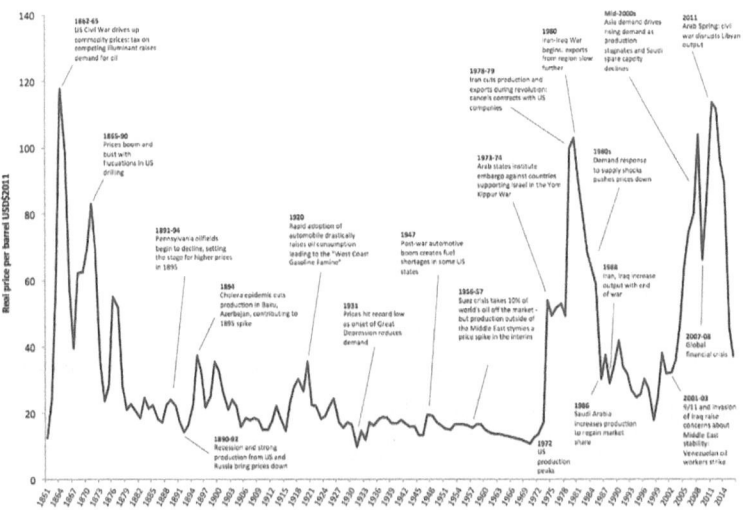

## Bond Markets/Fixed Income

Usually, there is an inverse relation between the stock/equity market and the prices of bonds.

If interest rises, prices fall and yields rise.

If interest falls, prices rise and yields fall.

## Real Estate

In the last forty-five years, there have been three major cycles in the real estate market:

1. 1972–1989
2. 1989–2007
3. 2007–2018

Each cycle has an average of about fourteen to sixteen years and has given an average return of 13–14 percent.

How does the real estate cycle work?

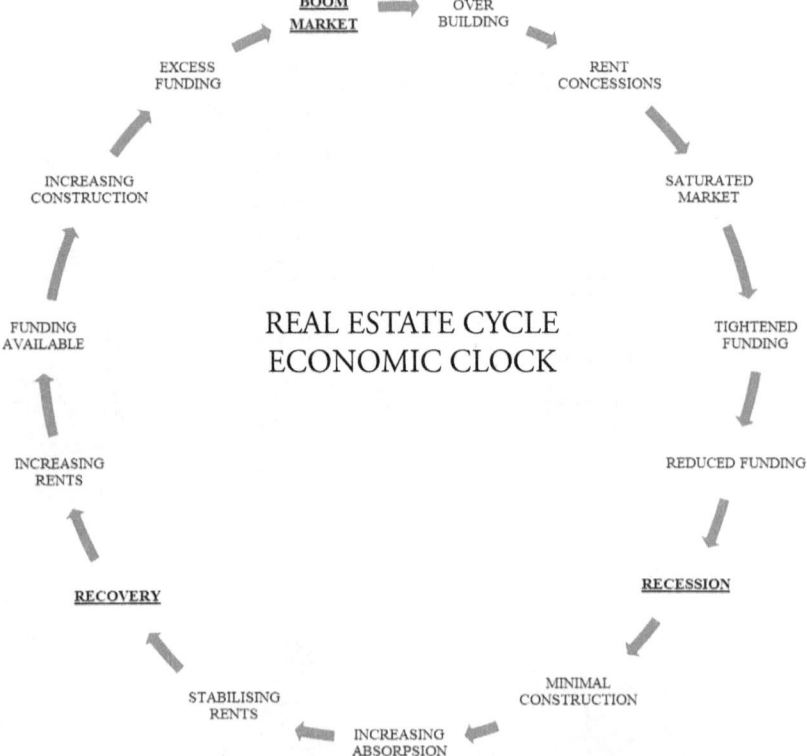

# The Subprime Crisis, 2007–2008

It occurred when banks sold too many mortgages to feed the demand for mortgage-backed securities through the secondary market, and when home prices fell in 2006 (real estate), it triggered a series of defaults. The ripple effect spread into mutual fund, pension's funds, and corporations who owned these derivatives and hence the ensuing banking crises in 2007–2008.

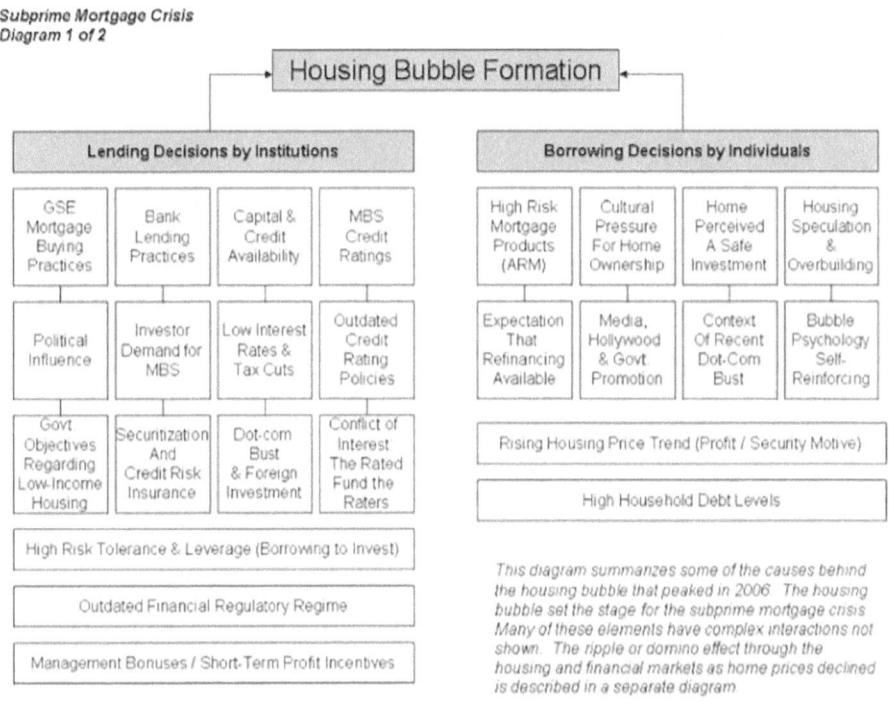

(Source: "Lending & Borrowing Decisions," 10/19/08. File: Subprime Crisis Diagram, X1.png, *Wikipedia*)

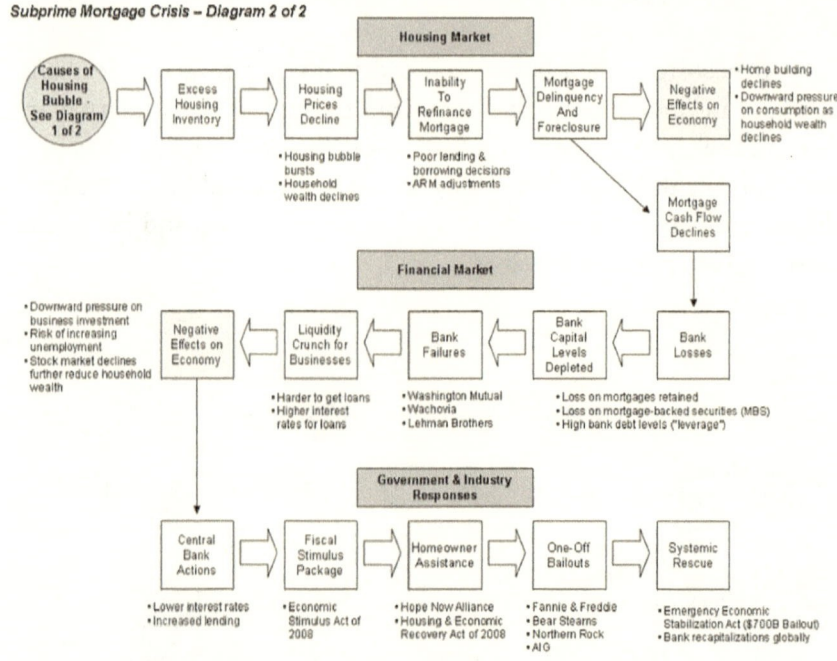

Subprime_Crisis_Diagram_-_X1.png
(960 × 720) (Source: Wikimedia.org)

The financial crisis produced the worst recession since the Great Depression. Thus, the fall of real estate, followed by equity markets, bonds markets, etc., eventually spread across countries.

# Chapter 6

# Why/How Do Countries
# Become Rich or Poor?

Countries' becoming rich or poor have been an outcome of the decisions by the policymakers of the countries that shape their economies, their successes, and their failures. All the aftereffects of these policy decisions go in making a history and a legacy of the people who shape the country's future. These decisions also throw in opportunities and signals as to how "Specunomics" and "Specumatics" come into play.

Let's look at countries that went from being rich to poor.

**Iran**
*1925–1979*

The country experienced a period of social changes, economic development, and state encouragement for industrial growth with a view of reducing dependence on imports. Tax reforms and trade policies attracted increased private investments in mining, construction, manufacturing, and oil exploration. The industries only focused on meeting the growing local demand. Agriculture that employed 90 percent of the labor force was kept out of the purview of economic reforms. The international trades were shored up with oil exports at the expense of agricultural and industrial exports. By 1977, 79 percent of the total government revenue was from oil exports. Lack of investments did not allow the growth of the agricultural, traditional, and semitraditional industries and the service sector like the oil sector.

*1979–present*

After the fall of the government due to the revolution in 1979, the new regime came in with new policies. The banks along with the industries including the National Iranian Oil Corporation were nationalized. After the breakout of Iran–Iraq war in 1980, 80 percent of businesses became state-owned. With the regime change also started the continuous series of world economic sanctions, thereby crippling the economy with the fall in agriculture, industrial, and oil export markets. Even the massive surge of oil prices to $145 could not help the economy back on its feet as the surge in prices were followed by equally massive fall in prices of crude oil to $25 during the financial crises of 2008. With continuous economic sanctions faced by the country, the GDP growth rate stands at -2 percent, which once was at a peak of 23 percent. A country completely shut out to the world export and financial markets is today forced to sign barter traders for oil in exchange for food and medicines, a country which by 1960 was a net exporter of agri-commodities and was a net importer of the same by 1990.

## Venezuela
*1913–1990*

Venezuela is a country which as an economy suffered downfall not because of prices of oil but more so with the manner in which the government spending was handled. The country became an oil economy after the discovery of oil in 1913. During the 1920s, the oil sector boomed with foreign investments in the exploration and production of oil. Since the 1960s and the 1970s, talks of nationalization of the oil industry slowed down the expansions in the sector by the foreign companies, and eventually, it was nationalized in 1976.

The production too fell from the peak of 1970 by 70 percent by the mid eighties. Mainly an oil economy, it faced a double whammy of nationalized oil sector and highly fluctuating oil prices from a relatively stable oil prices of $2/barrel in the 1970s to $12 during the oil shock of 1974, to $145 in the 2008, and to $25 during the 2008 financial crisis.

*1990–present*

After years of dictatorship, Hugo Chavez became the first president of the country in 1998. Increasing oil prices during the 2000s was unprecedented. The oil revenues were used by the president to retain political power through social programs. Social work of Chavez relied heavily on the oil money, and by 2010, with the collapse of oil prices, these social programs became unsustainable. Following Chavez's death in 2013, one of his cronies, Nicolas Maduro, became the president, hence continuing the same social programs with heavy external borrowings. By 2018, the inflation rates hit a high of 4000 percent. Today, the country is highly indebted where crude oil rights have been pledged to China for funding to run the country. The authoritarian rule and socialist economic policies of the government have plundered the natural resources of the country driving a once prosperous nation to economic ruin.

**Zambia**
*1928–1964*

In 1928, as enormous copper deposits were discovered, the country became known as the Copper Belt. By the year 1938, the country exported 13 percent of the world's copper. The sector was developed by two companies, the Anglo-American Corporation and the South African Rhodesian Trust, who controlled the sector till independence. In 1964, the country gained independence, and despite considerable mineral wealth, Zambia faced a major challenge as there were very few trained and educated Zambians capable to run the government and the economy, which was largely dependent on foreign expertise before independence.

*1964–2006*

After independence, the country adopted an ideology of socialism, where the economic policies focused on nationalization of the natural resources. By 1970, it took control of all the mining companies in the country. By the rising commodity prices, the country used all the proceeds from the copper gains to support the socialist government spending. Under state ownership, maintenance, and investments in the copper sector was completely neglected. In 1990, with the end of one president's rule, the new regime under its new policies called in private investments and sold back the mines to Anglo-American with sixty years of tax holidays at the lowest bid prices. Even after with the boom in copper prices in 2006 and with the copper deposits worth $1.4 trillion, it could have helped the country easily pay off one-third of its debts, but the super profits ended up in the hands of foreign-owned shareholders.

## Zimbabwe
*1980–2000*

Zimbabwe was once the bread basket of Africa. But industrial mismanagement, food shortages, corruption, and collapsed currency ruined the economy. After independence from the British in 1980, Robert Mugabe was elected the prime minister. For want of populist stance, he wanted to work for the people but with no interest for the economy. The nation steadily grew its exports of manufactured goods and agricultural goods. The country was famous for its tobacco production, and the weather supported year-round farming. As the Mugabe's popularity started fading by the nineties, he was accused of using brutality and bribery to maintain power, hence started the mismanagement of country's farming sector that contributed to an economic catastrophe. The government ended decades of farm ownership by white landlords, and land was redistributed to the local population with no knowledge of farming. By the 2000s, the agricultural output went down by 60 percent. There were food shortages, and this was aggravated by two years of drought leading to country's worst famine in sixty years.

*2000–present*

These shortages led to crisis, and the central bank ramped up money printing, resulting in rampant inflation. By 2008, economists estimated the inflation reached 7.9 billion percent. In 2008, the economy shrank by 18 percent, and in 2009, the country abandoned its currency and adopted the use of US dollars, South African, and seven other currencies to conduct business transactions. By 2010, the government shifted focus from farms to mines, and all the diamond mines were nationalized. Having been blessed with natural resources like coal, copper, iron ore, diamonds, and fertile land, and yet the country is still ruing under economic difficulties.

## Countries That Went from Being Poor to Rich

### Japan
*1946–1972*

Japan was seriously hammered during the Second World War. Post-war, the recovery of Japan is often called the "Japanese Economic Miracle." After the nuclear bombings on Japan in 1945, the country's industrial production decreased to 27.6 percent in 1946, but by 1960, it reached 350 percent, one of the reasons behind this was the successful economic reforms by the government. The second reason for Japan's rapid recovery after World War II was the outbreak of the Korean War. With the participation of America in the Korean War, it turned toward Japan for supplies of the required munitions and logistics to the American to fight the war. This resulted in rapid industrial growth. The rapid growth between 1955 to 1961 paved the way for the Golden Sixties, the decade that is generally associated with the Japanese economic miracle. In 1965, Japan's nominal GDP, estimated at just over $91 billion, reached to a record $1.065 trillion in a matter of fifteen years.

*1973–1992*

The oil crisis in 1973 and the second oil shock in 1978–1979 did affect the industrial production of Japan by 20 percent, but the country withstood the shocks and regained back by transforming itself from product-concentrating to technology-concentrating production form. The country moved toward more environmentally friendly production with less oil consumption. In 1985, the signing of the "Plaza Accord" was something that America wanted more as the growing Japanese economy was hurting American economic interests. The goal of the Plaza Accord was to weaken the US dollar in order to reduce the mounting US trade deficit. The Plaza Accord led to the yen and Deutsch mark dramatically increasing in value relative to the dollar. An unintended consequence of the Plaza Accord was that it paved the way for Japan's "Lost Decade" of sluggish growth and deflation.

## Singapore
*1965–1972*

Singapore gained its independence in 1965 from the British. After the World War II, the country had problems of high unemployment, slow economic growth, decaying infrastructure, and social unrest. But with the effective implementation of soundly conceived government policies with the right structural reforms, the economic progress was put on the right track. Industrialization through foreign direct investments by 1972, a quarter of the country's manufacturing firms were foreign owned or joint venture companies with United States and Japan both being major investors. This resulted in GDP growing double digits for most of the period from 1973 to 1975.

*1973–present*

The oil shock in 1973 and 1979 did put brakes on the super growth, which went as high as 15 percent but tumbled down to 8.7 percent between 1973 to 1979. But this rate was still high compared to other countries in the same period. By the late 1980, under the new economic policies of President Lee Kuan Yew, Singapore had become the world's largest petroleum refining center as well as the third largest oil trading center. By 1988, it pipped Rotterdam to be the busiest port in terms of tonnage. By 1990, the country's international banking and financial services was one of the fastest growing sectors, contributing 25 percent of the GDP. The government provided incentives for continuing diversification and automation of financial services. In 1997, Singapore's per capita income exceeded $33,000.

## Commodity Backbone for Rise and Fall of Countries

### Brazil: Ethanol and the Rise of an Economy

Sugarcane has been cultivated in Brazil since 1532 as sugar was one of the first commodities exported to Europe by the Portuguese settlers. The first use of sugarcane ethanol as a fuel in Brazil dates back to the late twenties and early thirties of the twentieth century, with the introduction of the automobile in the country. Ethanol fuel production peaked during World War II, and as German submarine attacks threatened oil supplies, the mandatory blend became as high as 50 percent in 1943. After the end of the war, cheap oil caused gasoline to prevail, and ethanol blends were only used sporadically, mostly to take advantage of sugar surpluses until the seventies, when the first oil crisis resulted in gasoline shortages and awareness of the dangers of oil dependence. As a response to this crisis, the Brazilian government began promoting bioethanol as a fuel. The National Alcohol Program, *Pró-Álcool* (Portuguese: *Programa Nacional do Álcool*), launched in 1975, was a nationwide program financed by

35

the government to phase out automobile fuels derived from fossil fuels such as gasoline in favor of ethanol produced from sugarcane.

The ever-rising crude oil prices made Brazil the largest exporter of ethanol to the world, which also gave rise to alternatives like corn being used by the US, and to beat the competition, the US being an importer of Brazilian ethanol, put tariffs on imports to promote domestic corn ethanol, making them more competitive even with higher production costs. Later, crude oil price corrections also put a spanner in the growth engine of the Brazilian economy, which faced recession during 2010 and 2011. Fall in oil prices in 2015 also hurt the country's oil exports, with oil being one of the primary export commodities.

## Ghana's Loss Is Cote D'Ivoire's Gain—The Cocoa History

GHANA, also known as the Gold Coast by its colonial name, was the world's largest producer of cocoa and although Ghana inherited this title on gaining independence in 1957, neglect of the industry by the government of Dr. Kwame Nkrumah eventually resulted in the loss of this preeminence. Subsequent regimes sought to revive the production of cocoa, but Ghana has never yet regained the dominant position that she occupied in the 1950s and early 1960s. The cocoa farmers were known to be relatively very rich, and as independence approached, Kwame Nkrumah sought popularity by promising to take the wealth of cocoa farmers and give it to the nation. So it is not surprising that on gaining power, the government kept low the prices of cocoa paid to farmers and added high taxes to boost national revenue, which eventually lead to farmers losing interest in cocoa production as fewer trees were planted and output fell. By this time, the countries such as Cote d'Ivoire, Indonesia, and Brazil were major cocoa producers and the world prices were kept low by this abundance.

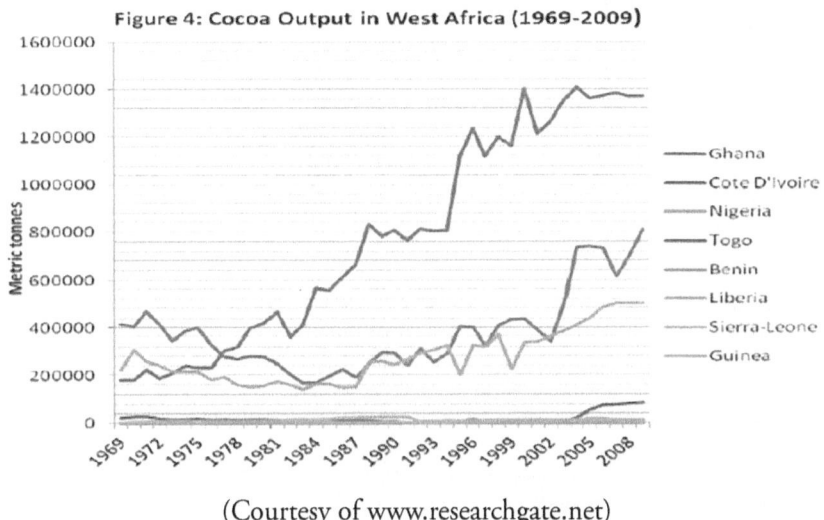

(Courtesy of www.researchgate.net)

It is quite visible how in 1978, Cote D'Ivoire overtook Ghana in cocoa production due to failed policies of the Ghanaian government, hence becoming the no. 1 ranking producer of cocoa in the world.

## China—The Rise of Superpower and Consumption Giant

Since the 1960s, China has lifted more than 800 million people out of poverty, as per capita GDP rose from $89 in 1960 to roughly $10000 today. The life expectancy has risen from 43.7 years in 1960 to 80 years today.

During 1979, Deng Xiaoping open-door policies started the real economic miracles. It was a mix of capitalism and communism. China, in a way, became the factory to the world consumption especially the United States and Europe. The large population was a boon to China's production boom in the way of cheap labor. The rising per capita income also gave rise to middle-class population in the country and consumption too. It used to be a saying at a time that "if China sneezes, the world catches cold." Such voracious was the infrastructure development in the country that it was consuming commodities from metals to energies to grain at an outpacing rate.

In fact, by 2022, China's 76 percent of urban population would be considered middle class. Today, 83 percent of China's payments are through mobile phones.

## China's Annual GDP Growth Since the 1970s

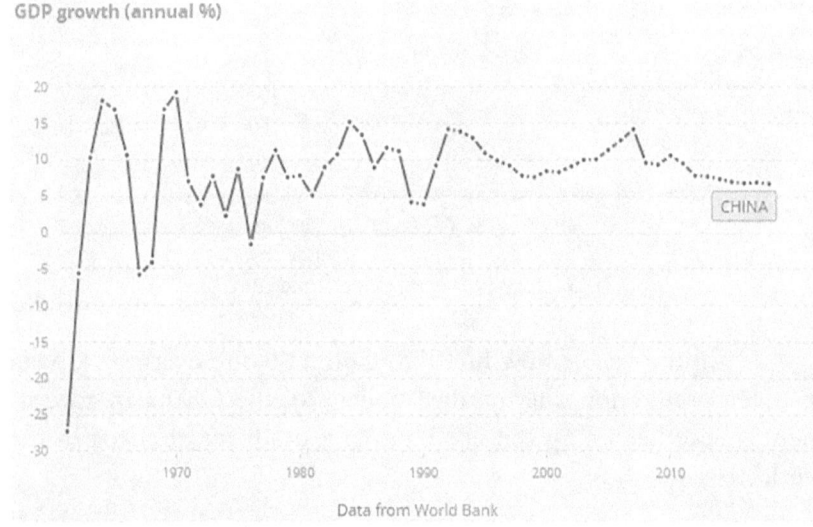

# Chapter 7

## When Alternatives/ Substitutes Become Mainframe Assets or Resources

1. **Vegelate—when chocolates go extinct in the next forty years**

   The term *VEGELATE* is a proposed term for chocolate containing vegetable oil instead of cocoa butter, the fat obtained from cocoa beans. Chocolate manufacturers around the world are now replacing cocoa butter to more evenly priced vegetable oil fats due to ever rising cocoa prices and global shortages of quality cocoa. Cocoa plants can only grow within a narrow strip of rainforests between twenty degrees north and south of the equator, which over a few decades could be endangered with rising temperatures by 2050. Half of the world's chocolates now come from only two countries within this belt—Cote d' Ivoire and Ghana. The not-so-encouraging government policies has cut the interest in cocoa cultivations in Cote d'Ivoire and ethical labor practices also have forced world intake of Ghanaian cocoa due to high use of child labor in cocoa cultivations. A cocoa crisis of this magnitude not only reduces the production of chocolates around the world but also raises the prices of chocolates, which may transform chocolates and its products in the luxury goods category.

2. **Ice cream—the melting industry**

With a growing consumer base toward health and hygiene products, rising cases of lactose intolerance and vegan movements are threatening the very existence of dairy-rich ice creams in the world today. The use of dairy substitutes has forced manufacturers to replace milk dairy fats with non-dairy extracts from coconut, almond, cashew, and soy (supposedly called vegetable milk extract). The global non-dairy milk market is projected to reach revenues of $40 billion by 2024, growing at an annual growth rate of 14 percent between 2018 and 2030.

3. **Coal and renewable energy (the American energy turnaround)**

Coal, which once was the benchmark for electricity generation in America, is rapidly being replaced with wind and solar plants all across, thus retiring most of the US power companies using coal for electricity generation. US power companies are expected to consume less coal than at any point since 1978. Global production of electricity too is recording a reduction of use of coal for electricity generation with a record decline in Germany, South Korea, and the first dip in three decades in India.

**Coal's shrinking role in powering America**
Power sector demand for coal is projected to drop in 2020 to the lowest level since 1978.

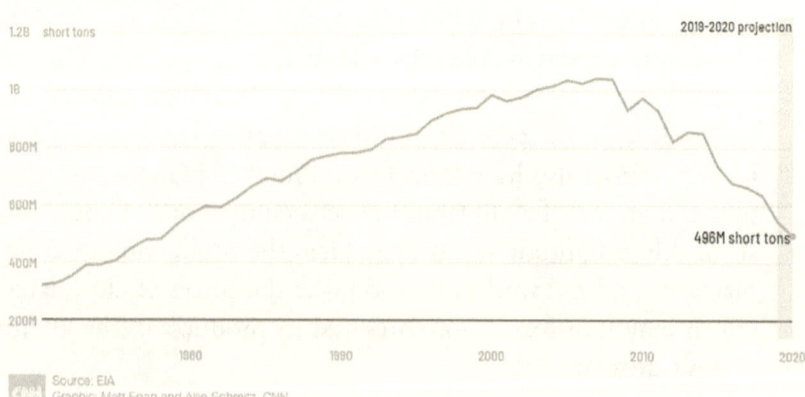

Source: EIA
Graphic: Matt Egan and Allie Schmitz, CNN

4. **HFCS (high-fructose corn syrup), a brief American history**

HFCS, a liquid fructose-based sweetener made from corn is commonly substituted for sugar in processed foods. It was introduced in the US food supply in 1970 due to escalating cane and sugar beet prices. Those costs have remained high because of US tariffs on sugar and corn farming subsidies, which makes HFCS cheaper to use than traditional sugar. HFCS was rapidly introduced into many processed foods and soft drinks in the United States from 1975 to 1985. In the 1980s, both Coke and Pepsi switched from fifty-fifty blend of sugar and HFCS to 100 percent HFCS, saving them 20 percent in sweetener cost.

Imports of sugar into the United States declined because of major policy restrictions in 1981 and 1996. In addition, the increase in the use of HFCS has displaced the import share of the sugar market. HFCS is used in almost every packaged food and soft drink American consumers see today. HFCS has replaced more expensively priced sugar in most of the industries, including the beverage industry (41 percent), processed food manufacturers (22 percent), cereal and bakery producers (14 percent), multiple-use food manufacturers (12 percent), the dairy industry (9 percent), and the confectionery industry (1 percent).

It was only since the 2000s that HFCS gained a bad name for contributing heavily in the rise of obesity in average Americans, and the shares of HFCS gradually have been taking a beating in the consumption share slumps. A substitute that could take its place will also take a matter of time.

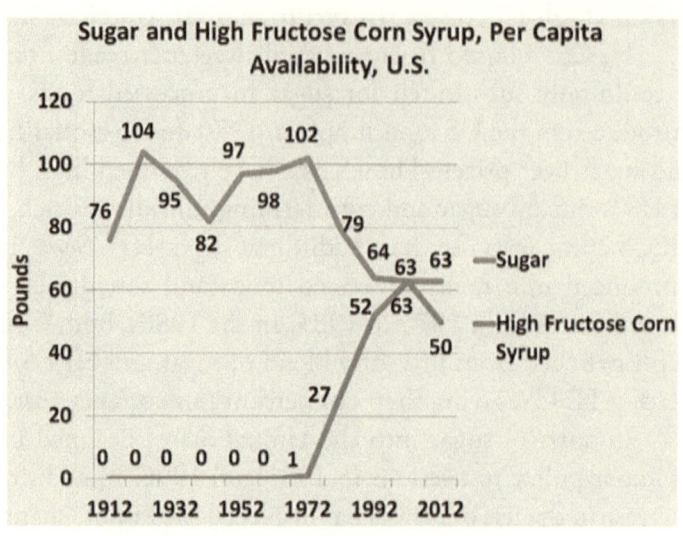

(Courtesy of www.ahundredyearsago.com)

## Per Capita Consumption of HFCS in the USA in 2000–2019 (in Pounds)

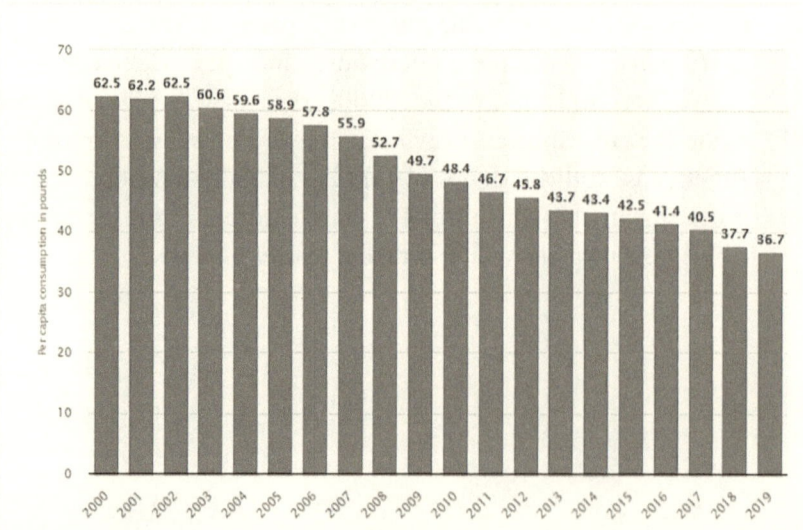

5. **Stevia**

Stevia or, as called in Sanskrit, *Madhur Patra*, is likely to be the greatest substitute to sugar. Stevia can be used as a "sweetener" for diabetic people without having any chemical in it like the artificial sweeteners commonly used. It is as natural as one can get.

Now as usage of stevia increases, one can see its disruption effect on sugar and its prices. Very important for a speculator to analyze from sugar companies to stevia manufacturing companies is where the stock picking decision goes.

### Market value of stevia worldwide from 2017 to 2022
*(in million U.S. dollars)*

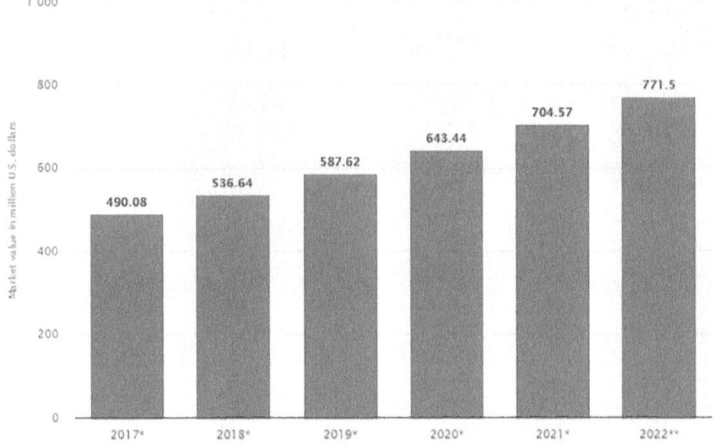

*Source: Stevia's Global Market Value, 2017–2022 | Statista*

6. **Cluster beans/guar seed**

US oil companies started drilling for oil in 2010 with a technology called hydraulic fracking, or fracking, which changed the whole dynamics of oil well drilling where it starts with vertical drilling and then goes horizontally deep and creates fissure internally in the oil deposits to pump out oil, which created a voracious appetite for a powder-like gum made from the seeds of guar or cluster beans, which created a bonanza for farmers in India, where 80 percent of the world supply for it comes from. A commodity till before the boom was used as a thickening agent in sauces and ice creams, which became the main ingredient for hydraulic fracking, thus starting the Shale Oil Boom for the United States, turning the country into a net exporter of oil from a net importer within a decade. This clearly reflected in the prices of cluster beans/guar seed shooting up eightfold within two years. With such a price rise, the demand for alternatives quickly filled in the markets like slick water, which overturned the whole boom in the cluster beans market within two years. The prices after those events never till today have been able to regain that past glory.

Thus, with the above deliberations, it is for us now to determine and evaluate whether we go into microeconomics or macroeconomics, depending on the asset class that needs to be analyzed, forecasted, and traded in order to make profits.

It is my proven conviction that as a discipline, it unravels historical trends, interprets today's situations, and makes predictions for the coming time.

# Chapter 8

# Economics Is Money

Why do we ignore information (data) that would help us to make better decisions?

Most people term this as OLD SCHOOL techniques, and I say it is the only way of thinking that lasts through times and ages to come. It trumps the high-frequency algorithm trades (HFT) as there are strong fundamental parameters that makes one visualize the future far beyond the basic concept of analysis:

1. **Prices**

    Prices determine the first basis of predicting any asset class.

    They're determinants of the CMP (current market price)—is it overvalued or undervalued or fairly priced?

    So from here, the process of analysis and number crunching commences.

2. **Sentiment**

    This is a great influencer to farmers in particular so as to decide what has to be grown in majority part of the farmlands, also to miners and explorers as cost benefit analysis is critical. Because beyond or below a particular price, the sentiment changes and also the patterns and movements, thus resulting in huge moneymaking opportunities (and so on to the industries that are either on the raw material side or the finished product side that has varying effects).

3. **Geography**

So here we analyze the world in spatial terms.

The effect of climate and weather on all asset classes—its influence is from crops to logistics.

- Correct reading of satellite images is crucial when it comes to agro-growth forecast
- Geological survey understanding when it comes to mining and exploration
- Location when it comes to placing an industry
- Logistical framework and infrastructure in consideration with all the above factors

4. **Inventories**

This is something that becomes common across the board for analyzing the movement or, in fact, stoppage of movement of the asset in various phases of a cycle.

From farmland produce pricing issues to industrial stock usage ratio, this becomes a very important tool in combination with others to forecast the coming big moneymaking opportunity.

5. **Demand/supply and production/consumption**

All four are heavily interlinked and keep influencing each other like a domino chain. But one has to note each in a distinct manner as they stand out too in major analysis and predictions independently.

6. **Substitutes and alternatives**

This usually is a commodity class feature, wherein when prices go beyond a range, there is always another commodity that can be replaced, thus resulting in a major shift in the cycles of our parameter 5.

7.  **A. Agro-specific**
      Data has to be accumulated of
      - soil conditions,
      - sowing progress,
      - crop growth progress,
      - harvest progress,
      - quality and yield, and
      - situations of all major producing and consuming countries need to be consolidated to have the macro view as well as the micro view to clearly trade the pattern that will be unfolding in the coming time.

    **B. Energy and metal related**
      Just like agro, it is again a very price-sensitive sector (the data here is a bit easy to come by).
      Geological survey understanding
      Cost escalations due to topography
      Quality and yield
      Logistical framework
      Geopolitical scenario specific to energy
      New inventions
      Environmental issues

    **C. Stocks**
      From A and B, one can analyze by linking data and forecasts to the industry and the companies involved in it. This always gives a better price projection of the companies as most conventional analysts do not take into account the fluctuations in the assets backing the corporate business.

8.  **Cultural beliefs also undermine the decision-making process**

    ## The Cannabis/Hemp Culture in America

    The Spaniards have been credited with the introduction of cannabis cultivation in the 1500s in America. Early cannabis cultivation provided fibers for making paper, rope, and numerous other products. Until the end of the 1800s, colonies were unaware of cannabis's psychoactive properties. Till the 1890s, physicians were recommending cannabis for medicinal uses. Later on, the Congress started regarding cannabis as narcotics, and by 1938, the federal government prohibited the use of cannabis. In 1989, President George Bush announced war on drugs. Finally, California set a precedent by the passage of proposition on legalization of sale of cannabis for medicinal uses. With the way legalization was sweeping all across the nation, several US states already allowed the use of cannabis for adult recreational purposes. By 2020, around thirty-six states have legalized medicinal use of cannabis.

Today, cannabis has become a multibillion industry, where it could be more than $35 billion industry. With information technology, the people are aware of the many uses and properties of hemp now.

Here are just a few creative products flooded in the markets:

- Cannabis skin care products
- Cannabis beverages
- Cannabis dog food
- Cannabis gummies antidepressant
- Cancer-related treatment

And many more...

These are the macro factors to impact the price movement of different asset classes.

In the coming chapters, we will see individual commodities' facets and their influence on various assets as well as asset classes.

# Chapter 9

## Crude Oil

The reason I have taken this as the first commodity to analyze is that its movement controls the economies of all the countries as well as a lot of industries that most are unaware of its indirect influence on the earnings and, eventually, the stock price.

As said, *"Knowledge is power"* and *"Power is in the barrels."*

And that will remain true as long as the use of oil is significant. Hence, until a complete revolution of renewable sources of energy happens, this fossil fuel will always affect the geopolitical economic events on this planet.

Here, we begin analyzing with OPEC, the official cartel created to manipulate prices. Individually, all countries denounce creation of cartels and syndicate bodies that try to influence monopolistic trade practices in various fields, but where OPEC is concerned, though its activities are internally denounced, yet all try to influence it in their favor.

| Non-OPEC Countries | OPEC Countries |
|---|---|
| Azerbaijan | Algeria |
| Brazil | Angola |
| Canada | Iran |
| Colombia | Iraq* |
| Kazakhstan | Kuwait |
| Mexico | Qatar* |
| Norway | Nigeria |
| Oman | Saudi Arabia |
| Russian Federation | United Arab Emirates |
| United Kingdom | Venezuela |

Source: International Trade Centre [20].

Where this book is concerned, we will stick to strong fundamental factors as whatever policies OPEC or other strong non-OPEC countries practice for us; our parameters will still lead to points from which decisions to make money are made.

So what we shall see from the periphery while analyzing oil are the following:

## Top Oil-Producing Countries

| Country | Million barrels per day | Share of world total |
|---|---|---|
| United States | 18.60 | 20% |
| Saudi Arabia | 11.01 | 12% |
| Russia | 10.50 | 11% |
| Canada | 5.29 | 6% |
| China | 4.93 | 5% |
| Iraq | 4.16 | 4% |
| United Arab Emirates | 3.79 | 4% |
| Brazil | 3.78 | 4% |
| Iran | 2.81 | 3% |
| Kuwait | 2.66 | 3% |
| Total top 10 | 67.52 | 72% |
| World total | 94.24 | |

(Source: International Energy Statistics, total oil [petroleum and other liquids] production, April 1, 2021)

## Top Oil-Consuming Countries

| Country | Million barrels per day | Share of world total |
|---|---|---|
| United States | 20.51 | 20% |
| China | 13.89 | 14% |
| India | 4.77 | 5% |
| Russia | 3.88 | 4% |
| Japan | 3.79 | 4% |
| Saudi Arabia | 3.08 | 3% |
| Brazil | 3.06 | 3% |
| South Korea | 2.57 | 3% |
| Canada | 2.53 | 3% |
| Germany | 2.33 | 2% |
| Total top 10 | 60.40 | 60% |
| World total | 100.37 | |

(Source: International Energy Statistics, total oil [petroleum and other liquids] consumption, December 1, 2020)

# Average Cost to Produce One Oil Barrel in Top Production Countries Worldwide (in US Dollars Per Barrel)

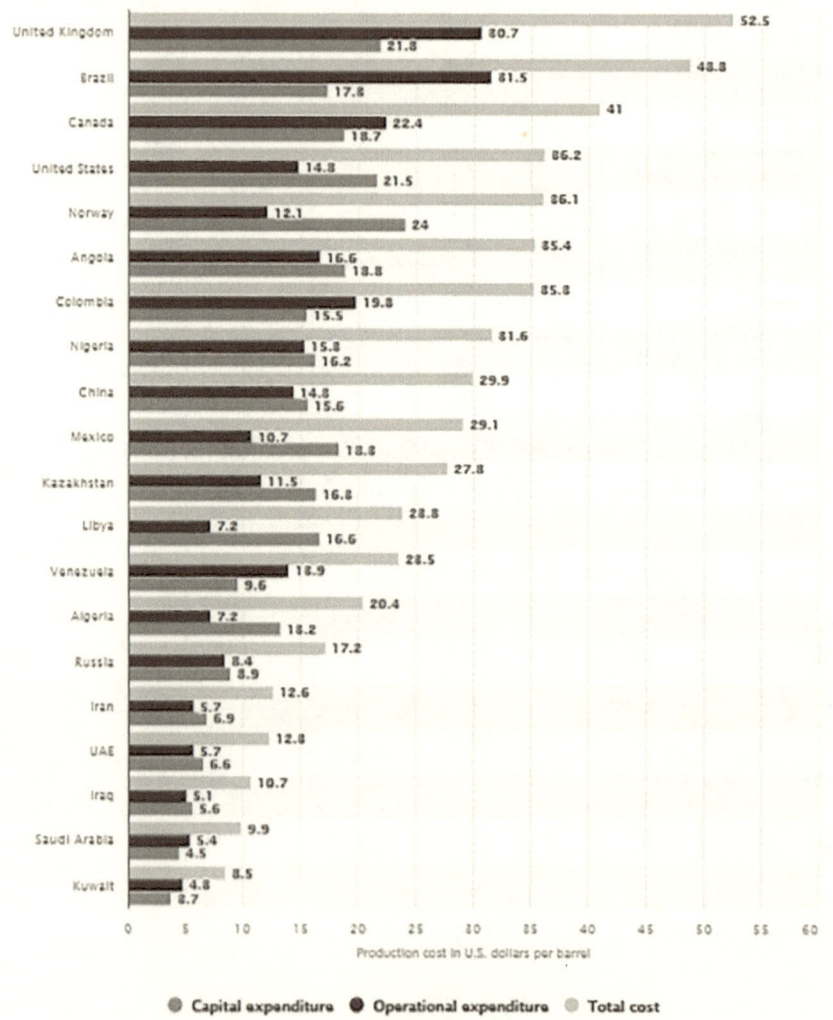

● Capital expenditure ● Operational expenditure ○ Total cost

(Source: Production cost breakdown per barrel of oil in top oil-producing countries 2015, *Statista*)

## Oil Produced Onshore or Offshore and Cost Variations Distribution of World Crude Oil, Onshore and Offshore Production

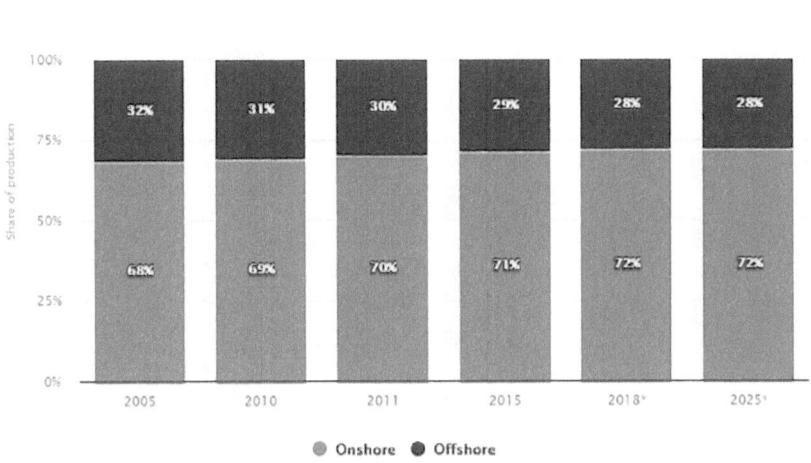

(Source: Global crude oil onshore and offshore production distribution 2025, *Statista*)

Now, though, some data is provided to get an idea, but all information is readily available on the search engines. My objective is to bring the macro factors to the forefront on the basis of which a person can begin the analysis and eventually comprehend the commodity, the movement, and further, the companies that get influenced by it. The ultimate aim for the reader is to make informed decisions based on certain parameters and speculate to earn money.

Any external disturbance in the Middle East, like the Iran–Iraq war, Saudi Arabia–Qatar standoff, or the Saudi Arabia–Iran tussle will result in RISK premium rocketing, and so will the prices of crude.

The very recent Suez Canal blockade in 2021 for six days from where 40 percent of world's oil tanker pass—any breakage in its free flow of movement resulted in rise of oil prices.

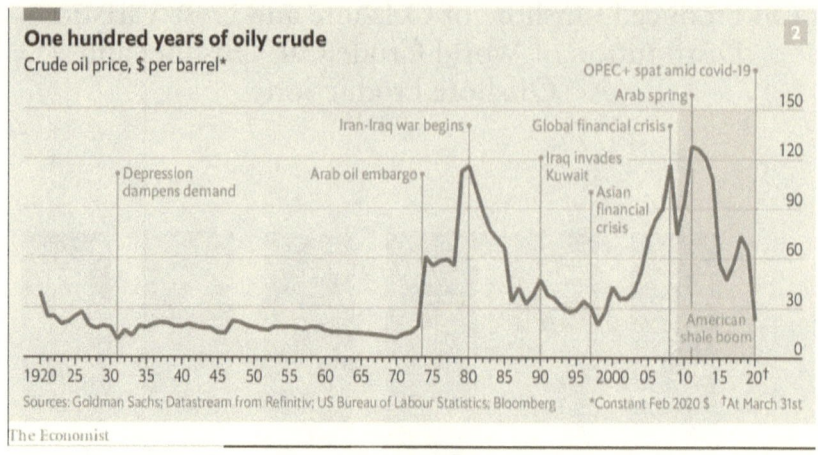

One hundred years of oily crude
Crude oil price, $ per barrel*

Sources: Goldman Sachs; Datastream from Refinitiv; US Bureau of Labour Statistics; Bloomberg    *Constant Feb 2020 $   †At March 31st

The Economist

## Crude Oil Monthly Chart

(Courtesy of www.investing.com)

Now this was how the world was till the shale oil revolution took place. USA, which used to be an importer of over nine million barrels some years ago with this oil coming and change in its own oil exploration policies during the Obama government, soon became an exporter, and this rebalanced the global demand-supply situation, resulting in a major fall in prices.

Of course, whether it's OPEC or non-OPEC, producers and even the shale oil producers would always prefer the prices to remain high, but the technology of extracting oil is bringing a new normal to the pricing of oil. And as the tech revolution in exploration continues, the ex-well cost is likely to reduce, thus bringing the prices of oil much lower and keeping the margins of the companies exploring it intact with a hedging mechanism. The reason to bring the previous statement is important as how we take our decision to invest in companies involved in oil exploration even during falling product prices is crucial.

So no matter what factors come into effect, we will stick to our economic principles only.

Total Production-Total Consumption = **Inventory**

As these figures keep moving daily and weekly and news flows like Nigerian rebels attack a refinery or Libyan internal problems reducing crude exports or Venezuela political imbroglio make its production negligible, we will still do data crunching of the numbers to continuously see how production has gone up or down and eventually what is likely inventory.

The demand/consumption factor is a significant future point as EVs revolution comes in.

**Long-term oil demand by region**                     *mb/d*

|  | 2019 | 2020 | 2025 | 2030 | 2035 | 2040 | 2045 | Growth 2019–2045 |
|---|---|---|---|---|---|---|---|---|
| OECD Americas | 25.6 | 23.3 | 25.7 | 24.8 | 23.1 | 21.2 | 19.3 | −6.3 |
| OECD Europe | 14.3 | 12.6 | 13.7 | 12.9 | 12.0 | 11.1 | 10.2 | −4.1 |
| OECD Asia Oceania | 7.9 | 7.1 | 7.4 | 6.9 | 6.4 | 5.8 | 5.2 | −2.7 |
| OECD | 47.9 | 43.0 | 46.8 | 44.6 | 41.5 | 38.0 | 34.8 | −13.1 |
| Latin America | 6.2 | 5.8 | 6.6 | 7.1 | 7.4 | 7.6 | 7.9 | 1.6 |
| Middle East & Africa | 4.3 | 3.9 | 4.8 | 5.5 | 6.2 | 6.9 | 7.6 | 3.3 |
| India | 4.8 | 4.3 | 5.8 | 7.2 | 8.6 | 9.9 | 11.1 | 6.3 |
| China | 13.1 | 12.1 | 14.4 | 15.5 | 16.2 | 16.7 | 17.1 | 4.0 |
| Other Asia | 9.0 | 8.5 | 9.9 | 10.9 | 11.7 | 12.4 | 13.0 | 3.9 |
| OPEC | 8.7 | 8.2 | 9.5 | 10.5 | 11.3 | 11.7 | 11.7 | 3.0 |
| Russia | 3.6 | 3.2 | 3.7 | 3.8 | 3.8 | 3.8 | 3.7 | 0.1 |
| Other Eurasia | 2.0 | 1.8 | 2.1 | 2.2 | 2.3 | 2.3 | 2.3 | 0.2 |
| Non-OECD | 51.8 | 47.8 | 56.9 | 62.6 | 67.4 | 71.2 | 74.3 | 22.5 |
| World | 99.7 | 90.7 | 103.7 | 107.2 | 108.9 | 109.3 | 109.1 | 9.4 |

*Source: OPEC.*

**OECD oil demand by sector, 2019–2045**

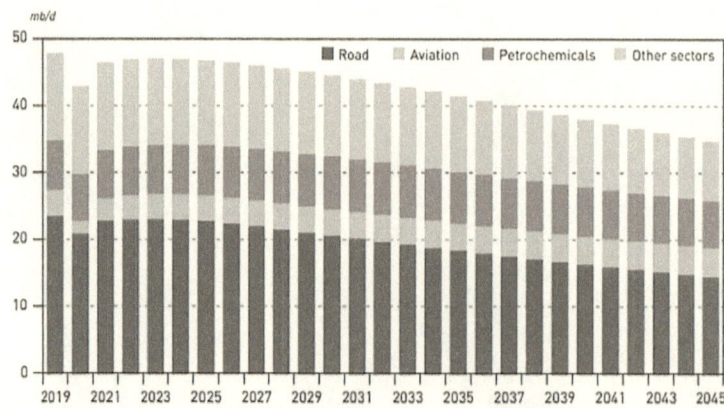

*Source: OPEC.*

56

Composition of the global vehicle fleet, 2019–2045

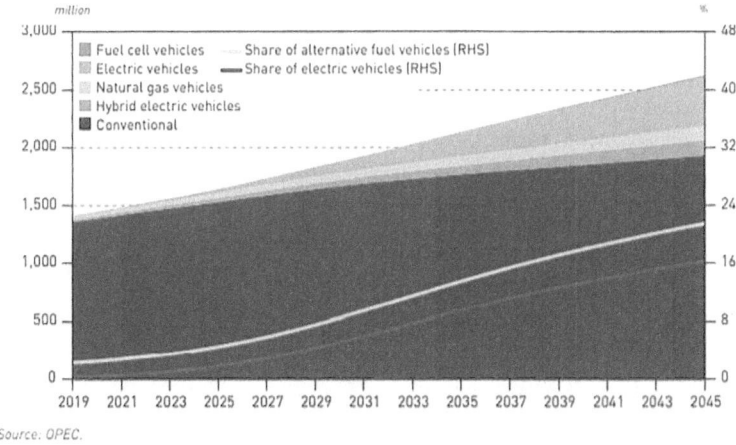

Source: OPEC.

## Electric vehicle sales

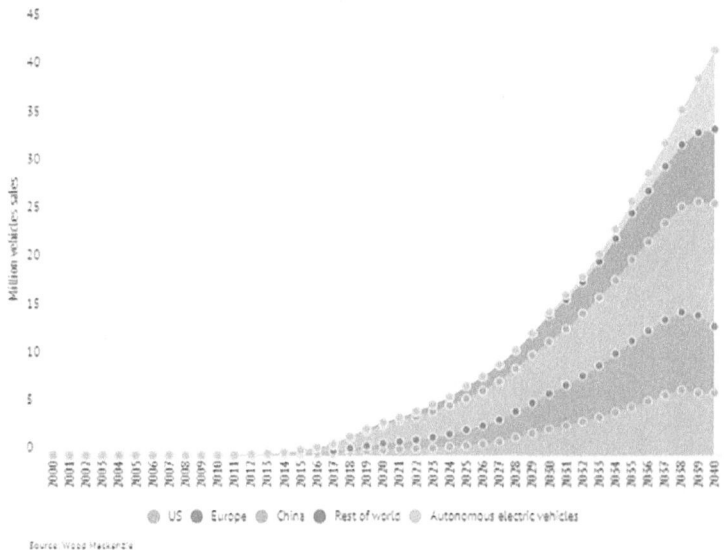

Now even if crude production peaks, there are times when a commodity or a product can force demand destruction and this factor is very crucial in analyzing the future price movements as this is also called as the substitution effect in economics.

So here the speculators' mind has to work in two directions to earn money:

1.   to make profits from fall in crude oil prices
2.   to make money from that commodity/product that is going to rise in terms of demand

Now these are the companies that are involved in crude.

## Exploration Companies

It is obvious that the higher the prices of crude, the higher the earnings, provided they can keep their costs too under control. Now many of these companies are smart hedgers during phases when crude prices have either remained stable or collapsed, so they can still cover up their production cost losses against the hedging through futures and options strategies.

Exxon Mobil Monthly Chart

(Courtesy of www.investing.com)

## Royal Dutch Shell Monthly Chart

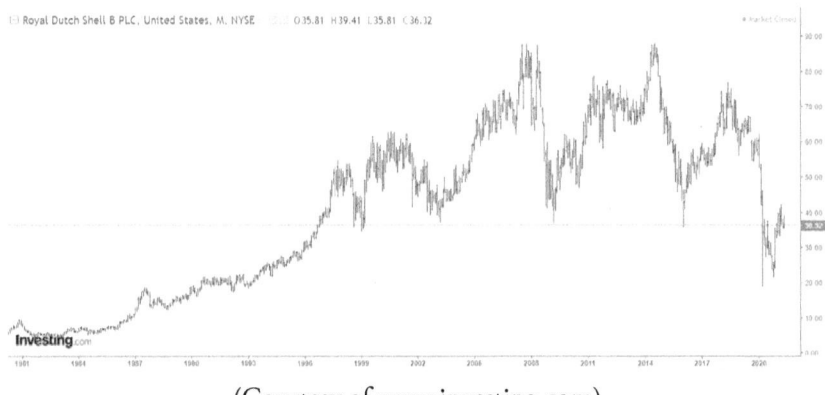

(Courtesy of www.investing.com)

## BP Monthly Chart

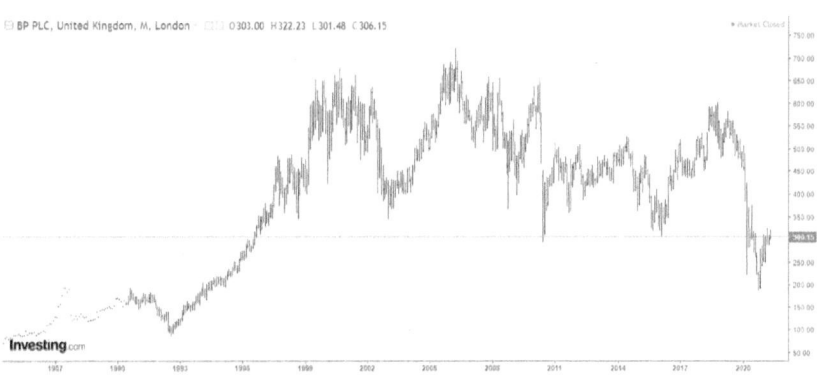

(Courtesy of www.investing.com)

## Petronas Monthly Chart

(Courtesy of www.investing.com)

## Diamondback Energy Monthly Chart

(Courtesy of www.investing.com)

Apache Monthly Chart

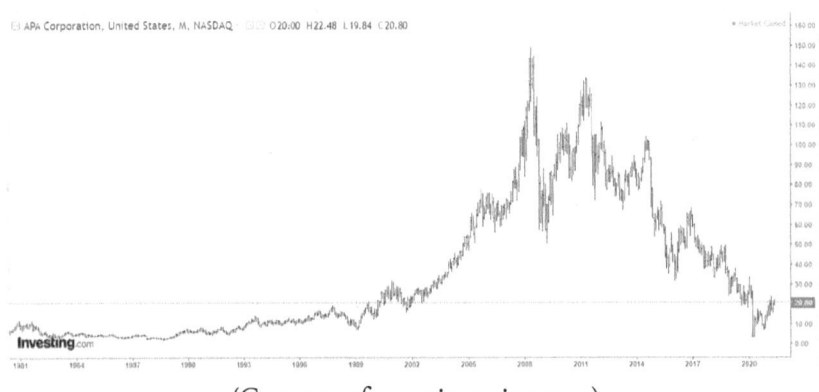

(Courtesy of www.investing.com)

# Refiners

Sinopec Monthly Chart

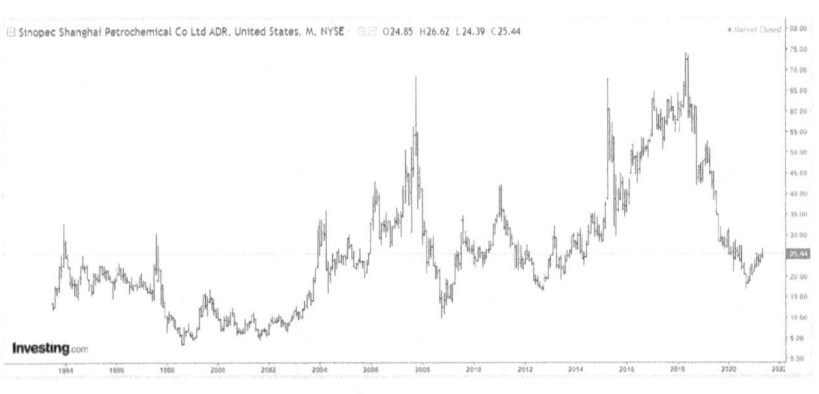

(Courtesy of www.investing.com)

# Pipeline Companies

These companies create the arteries and veins so a smooth flow of crude is maintained. And as more wells come up and go off, they need to keep building new infrastructures and maintaining the old as suddenly one day, the technology or price is such that an old well can become changeable.

Kinder Morgan Monthly Chart

(Courtesy of www.investing.com)

As business improves, the chart shows the movement in its price. They earn on the basis of per gallon flow, and it becomes significant to the shareholders as these companies are known to declare monthly dividends.

## Technology and Rig Construction Companies

Drilling tunnels from just one vertical downside it became feasible with two shoots forming that could start drilling horizontal too from under the surface so no digging another well from the top. This considerably reduced the cost of oil production. Hence such companies become a buy or sell depending on their further innovations as well as how long crude/ gas continue its global domination.

Baker Hughes Monthly Chart

(Courtesy of www.investing.com)

# Fertilizer Companies

Now one would think how crude oil and fertilizer get related. It's very simple. Most of the fertilizer producers used naphtha as their fuel; that is a byproduct of crude oil. But in the last couple of years, as the world moves toward greener environment with the carbon emission footprint reduction, there is a substitution happening. Natural gas is replacing naphtha as a cleaner fuel. We look at natural gas a bit later in the coming chapter.

So it is now that the natural gas pricing will affect the cost of producing fertilizers. The demand that is to happen due to agriculture growth and soil situations (to be discussed soon) also affects the earnings of these companies.

Let us see the price charts of the world's top fertilizer companies.

## Agrium (Post Merger with Potash Corp)—Nutrien Monthly Chart

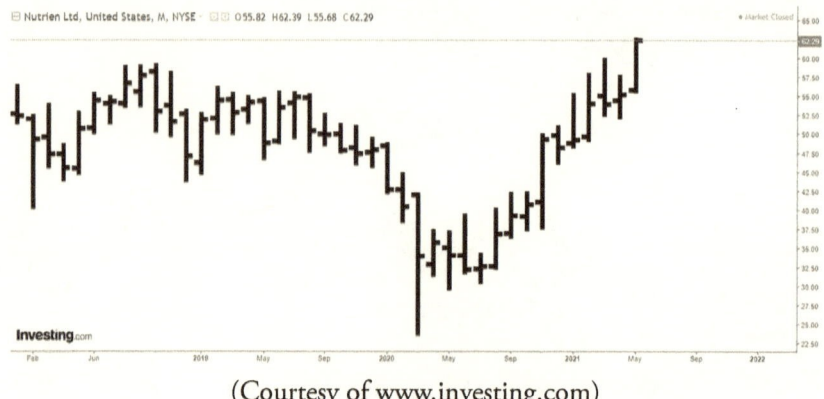

(Courtesy of www.investing.com)

## The Mosaic Company Monthly Chart

(Courtesy of www.investing.com)

Yara International Monthly Chart

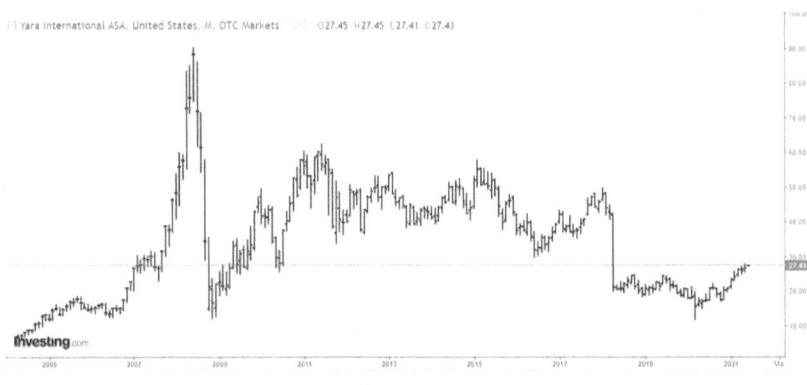

(Courtesy of www.investing.com)

Israel Chemicals Monthly Chart

(Courtesy of www.investing.com)

## Plastic Companies

Your plastic furniture to storage boxes (Tupperware) is dictated by the price of crude oil. So the higher the prices of crude oil, and if these companies have not hedged themselves in a long-term contract at a better price, the higher their costs will run, making their profitability fall and vice versa.

## Tupperware Monthly Chart

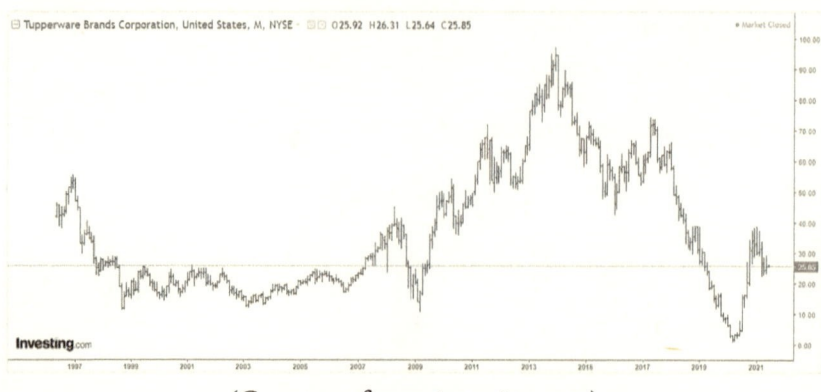

(Courtesy of www.investing.com)

Let us see the price charts of the world's top plastic companies.

## Dow Chemicals Monthly Chart

(Courtesy of www.investing.com)

## Lyondell Basell Monthly Chart

(Courtesy of www.investing.com)

## Sabic Monthly Chart

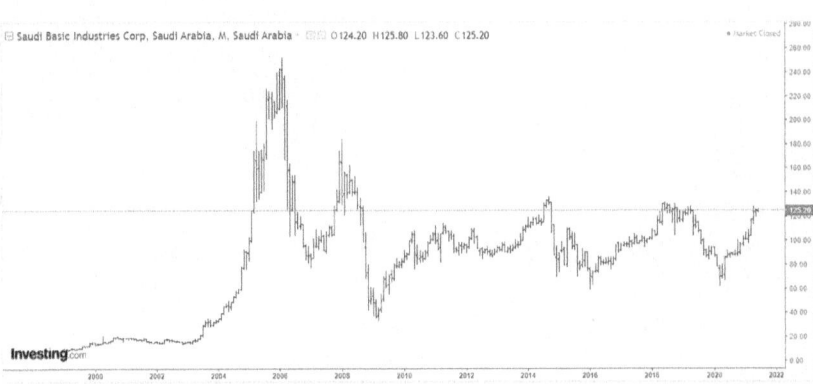

(Courtesy of www.investing.com)

## BASF Monthly Chart

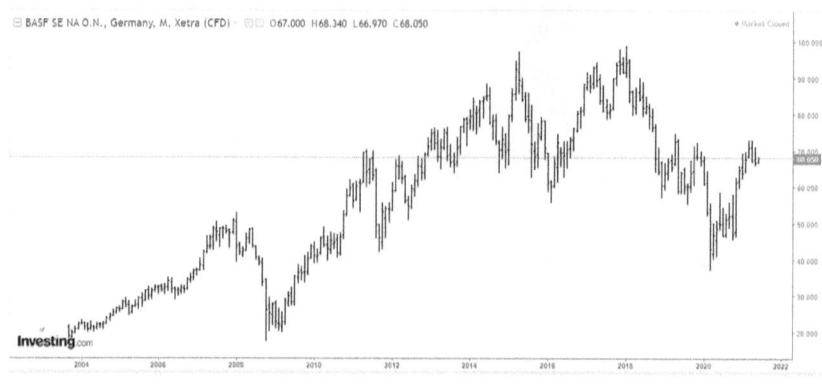

(Courtesy of www.investing.com)

## LG Chemicals Monthly Chart

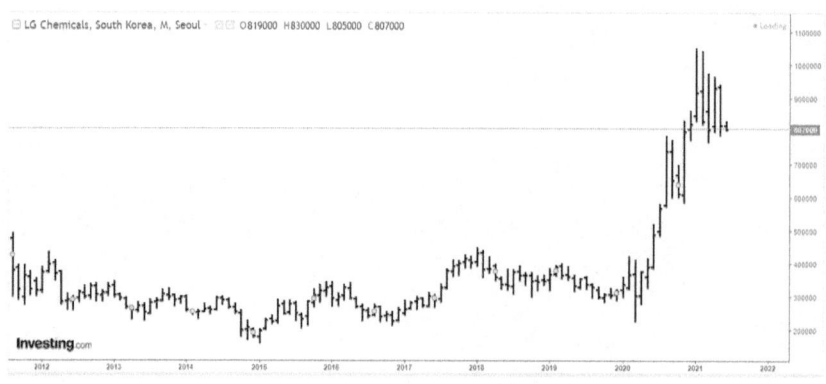

(Courtesy of www.investing.com)

## Lanxess Monthly Chart

(Courtesy of www.investing.com.)

## Formosa Plastics Corporation Monthly Chart

(Courtesy of www.investing.com)

# Specialty Chemicals

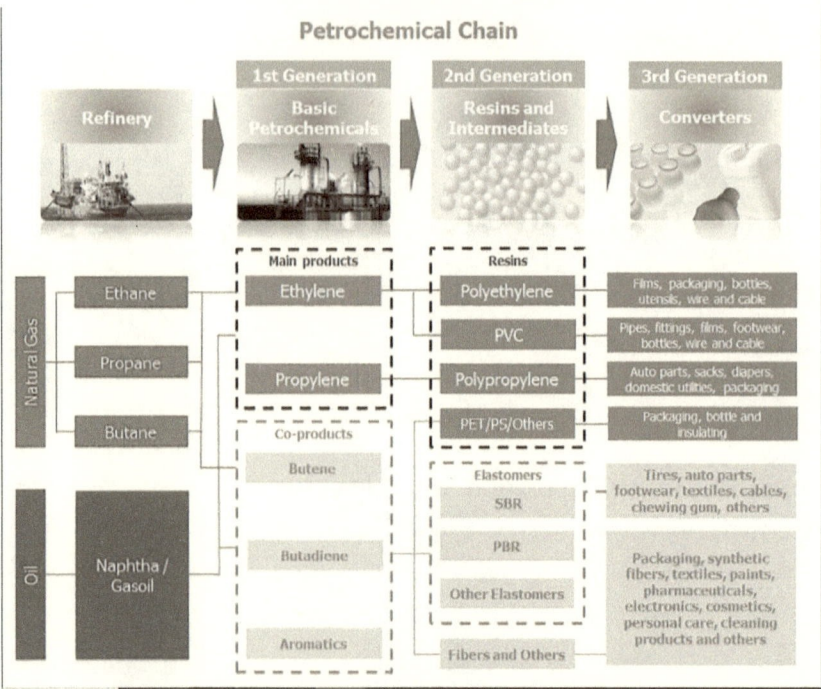

(Source: "Petrochemical Products—Durable
Engineering & Procurement," Depuk.co.uk)

Examples of a Few Specialty Chemicals

1.  Bitumen

     Bitumen, also known as asphalt in the United States, is a substance produced through the distillation of crude oil that is known for its waterproofing and adhesive properties. The material is used most often in road paving. The majority of roads are made of either bitumen or a combination of bitumen and aggregates, such as concrete.

Bitumen Price (China) Chart

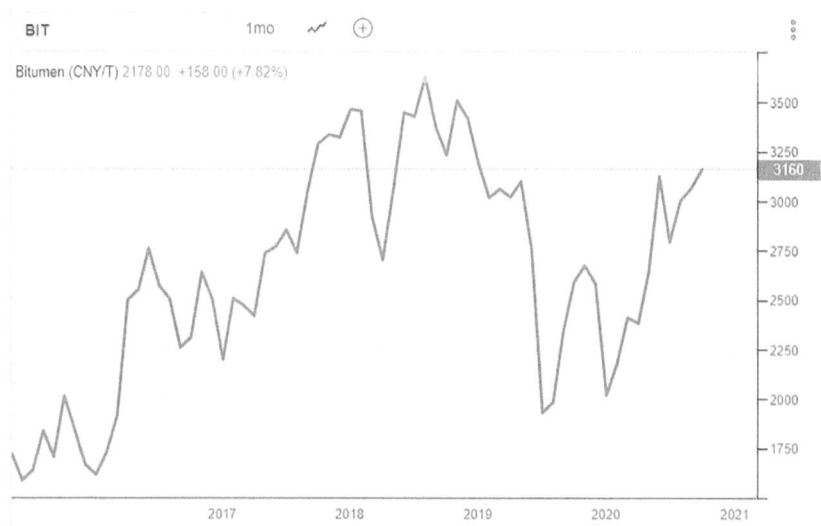

(Courtesy of www.investing.com)

2.  Benzene

    Benzene is found in crude oils and as a by-product of oil-refining processes. In the industry, benzene is used as a solvent, as a chemical intermediate, and in the synthesis of numerous chemicals. Industries use benzene to make other chemicals, which are used to make plastics, resins, and nylon and synthetic fibers. Benzene is also used to make some types of rubbers, lubricants, dyes, detergents, drugs, and pesticides.

Benzene Monthly Chart

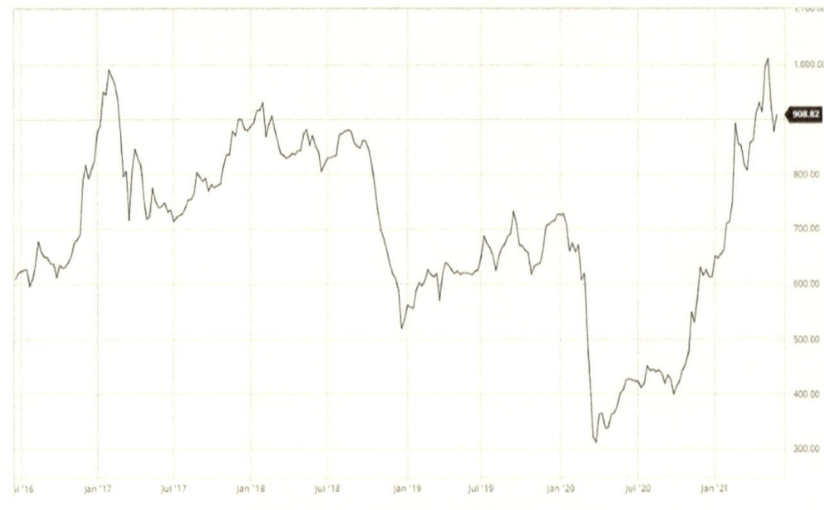

(Courtesy of www.barchart.com)

## Summarization

So what I am putting forth is that even before the financial statements are seen, the previous movement of crude and its projection of the future movement is analyzed for one to take a macro-view of how the industry is likely to be positioned. This itself is 60 percent of the decision-making analysis. The balance is through analyzing the company financials and how it is likely to perform on the basis of its product pricing factors with its own strengths and weakness present.

# Chapter 10

## Natural Gas

Let me reiterate once again that the purpose of this book is not to go into in-depth analysis, but rather, it to be used as a handbook for people of any walk of life to refer and make it a starting point of their analysis, to open their mind to this world where money can be made.

One of my mentors used to always say, "THE MARKETS ARE LIKE A CASH MINE. EVERY DAY, YOU TAKE YOUR BUCKET AND SHOVEL AND COLLECT HOW MUCH EVER YOU WANT TO." And this handbook can be one of the instruments in the sequences of analysis to make you a successful speculator.

### World's Top 5 Countries with Highest Natural Gas Production

| RANKING | COUNTRY | PRODUCTION (BILLION CUBIC METERS) |
|---------|---------|-----------------------------------|
| 1 | Russia | 47,805 |
| 2 | Iran | 33,721 |
| 3 | Qatar | 24,702 |
| 4 | US | 15,484 |
| 5 | Saudi Arabia | 9,200 |

(Source: "Natural Gas by Country 2021," worldpopulationreview.com)

## World's Top 5 Countries with Highest Natural Gas Consumption

| RANKING | COUNTRY | CONSUMPTION (million m³/year) |
|---|---|---|
| 1 | US | 846,600 |
| 2 | EU | 469,600 |
| 3 | Russia | 444,300 |
| 4 | China | 307,300 |
| 5 | Iran | 223,600 |

(Source: https://en.wikipedia.org)

Though the cracking and exploring process of crude results in many types of by-products and derivatives, we will focus on main ones and be with the macro aspects that aid our decision-making process.

Apart from just the direct and indirect use of natural gas, the pipeline industry also gains a lot that helps in the distribution of gas in various forms, the most common being liquefied petroleum gas (LPG) or cooking gas.

Liquefied natural gas, or LNG, is a major industry and process through which it is exported around the globe. And usually the benchmark calculator is the Japan Korea Marker (JKM), platts as is the commonly used term, and is usually double the prices of natural gas.

1. The prices of gas affect many industries like fertilizer, chemicals, etc. that become a part of their cost of production.
2. Also, severe temperatures result in usage of more gas for heaters, thus influencing the inventory-usage ratios.

So all in all, basic economic principles, or what we call eco equations, come into picture as to how the surpluses and deficits are in place.

It is very evident from the charts below that the rise in natural gas prices results in a super run up for gas companies.

## Nymex Natural Gas Monthly Chart

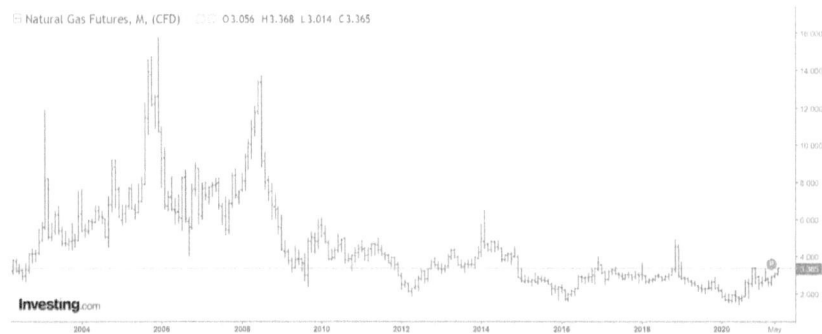

(Courtesy of www.investing.com)

## JK Marker Monthly Chart

(Courtesy of www.tradingview.com)

## Cheniere Energy Monthly Chart

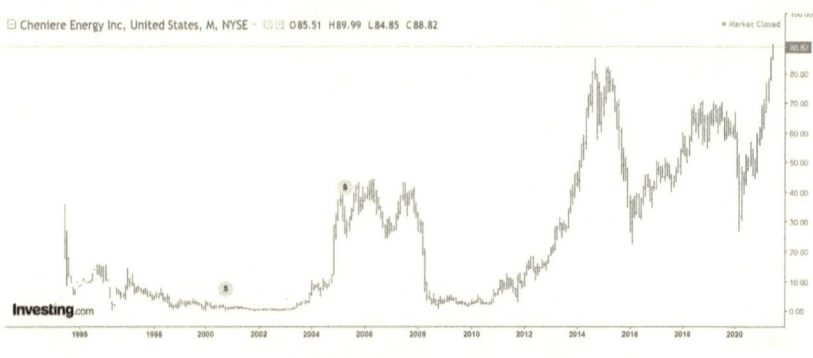

(Courtesy of www.investing.com.)

## Gazprom Monthly Chart

(Courtesy of www.investing.com)

Tellurian Monthly Chart

(Courtesy of www.investing.com)

## Summarization

With a certain time lag, the natural gas-producing companies follow the commodity. The comparison is clear as first, the sentiment always makes the move, and then the financials of the company have to be studied to understand how much earnings they are likely to improve or lose depending on the move.

# Chapter 11

## Sugar

The reason I have brought up sugar immediately after the energies is that I consider sugar as an energy commodity as high-quality ethanol is produced from the cane that has become a clean energy source. Other countries are a bit slow in catching up with this fuel like India and Europe due to the strong political lobbies as well as the powerful crude oil lobbies who can see their dominance getting diminished if ethanol is completely freed up to be used as the driving fuel.

Hence, they regulate and control it to keep it as a blend and earn brownie points through this eye washing of the general populace.

### World's Top Producers of Sugar

| RANKING | COUNTRY | MILLION METRIC TONS |
|---------|---------|---------------------|
| 1 | Brazil | 29.93 |
| 2 | India | 28.9 |
| 3 | The EU (Beet Sugar) | 17.25 |
| 4 | China | 10.2 |
| 5 | Thailand | 8.25 |

(Source: www.investopedia.com)

## World's Top Consumers of Sugar

| RANKING | COUNTRY | MILLION METRIC TONS |
|---------|---------|---------------------|
| 1 | India | 25.51 |
| 2 | EU-28 | 18.11 |
| 3 | China | 16.20 |
| 4 | Brazil | 10.55 |
| 5 | USA | 10.24 |

(Source: www.isosugar.org)

The cycle of cane growing is approximately fifteen months. The long gestation period results in enormous volatility and hedging in sugar prices around the world.

It is said that sugar is sweet, while speculating it can leave a bitter taste. But reading ahead, I will try my best to reduce that probability to negligible.

So to come to our effective decision-making data, we need to understand the farmer sentiment and how lucrative it is to grow sugarcane in the coming long season, taking into account the pricing estimates globally and locally.

For a commodity speculator, he will have to check on the soil conditions (as mentioned in one of the previous chapters), the vagaries of rains, underground water levels and its addition or depletion, arable area this time as cane is growing to check on its girth for yield purposes, and eventually, the change in pricing as we near the harvest season. As all these figures are collected and summarized from around the world, we will come to a conclusion as to the final inventory or stock and how the price shall move for the speculators to make the profits.

The pricing in this period also is determined by the crude oil prices. If they are high, the Brazilians tend to shift cane from sugar to ethanol production, making sugar prices rise in proportion to the shift and vice versa.

Where the stock investor is concerned, his working starts from the ex-mill prices of sugar and its movement based on inventory kept by the sugar companies. How these sugar companies are able to hedge or sell their product at future prices is crucial to arrive at these companies' abilities and so the forecast of their EPS.

I firmly believe that with all combined, a person stands a distinct advantage as one can take benefit of first making money through sugar's future contract trading in both directions as needed and then through sugar company stock investments or shorting or selling futures as the data and movement evolve.

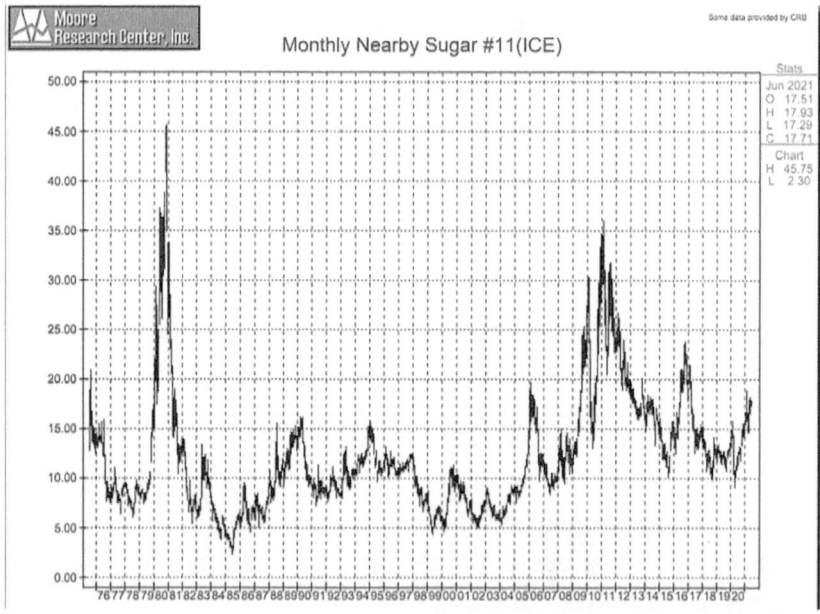

Cosan Ltd.

Cosan is a public listed company, a Brazilian conglomerate producer of bioethanol, sugar, and energy.

## Cosan Monthly Chart

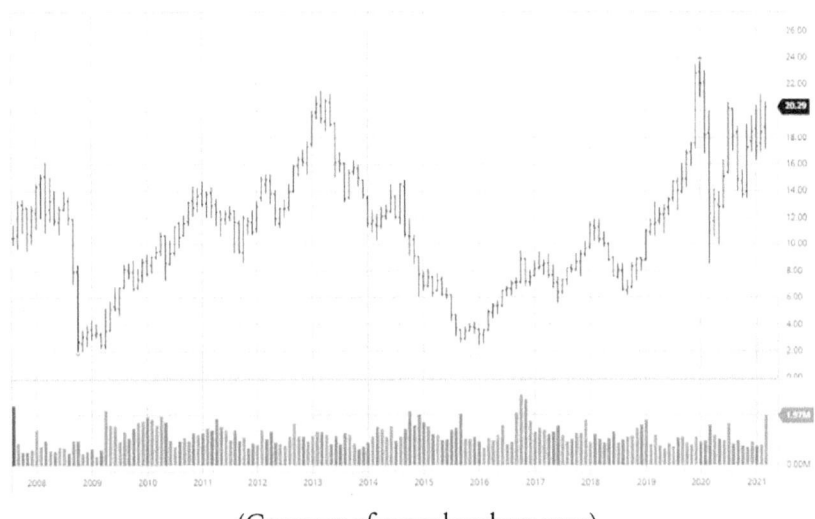

(Courtesy of www.barchart.com)

## Ethanol Monthly Price Chart

(Courtesy of www.businessinsider.com)

## Ethanol and Crude Oil Price Relation Chart

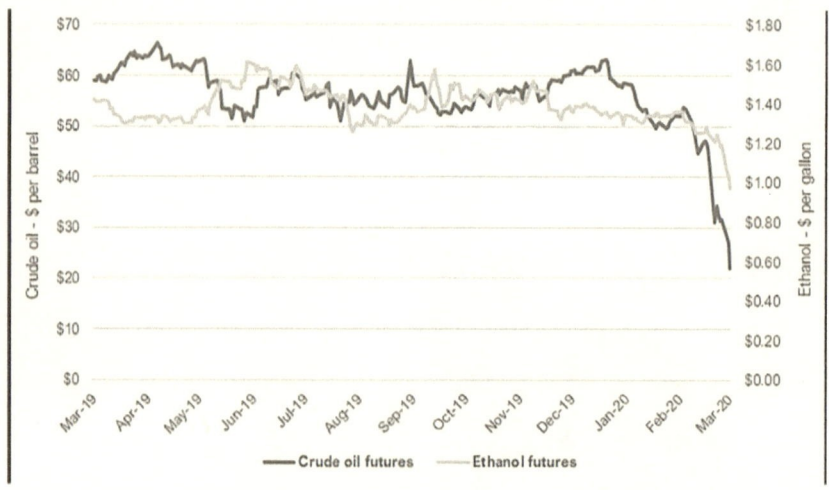

(Courtesy of www.mckeany-flavell.com)

## Coca-Cola Monthly Chart

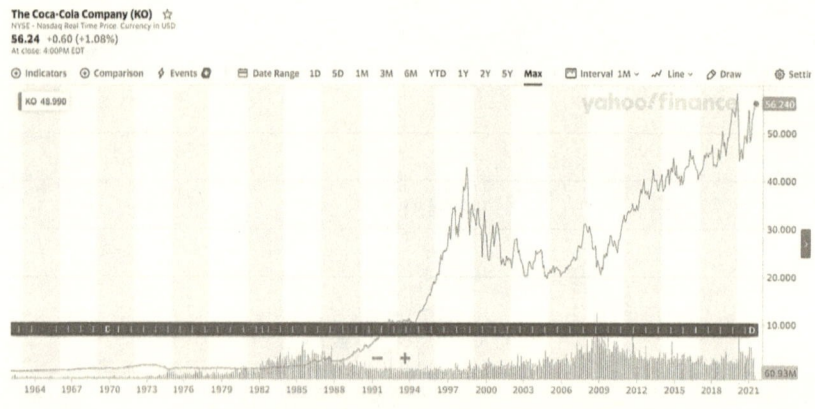

(Courtesy of www.yahoofinance.com)

It is evident from the above charts as the sugar prices fall, the profitability of Coca-Cola rises, resulting in the price rise.

Fresh Del Monte Monthly Chart

(Courtesy of www.investing.com)

Sugarcane crushing first results in raw sugar, and as it is decarbonized and refined, then we have the white sugar.

## The Sugarcane Refining Process

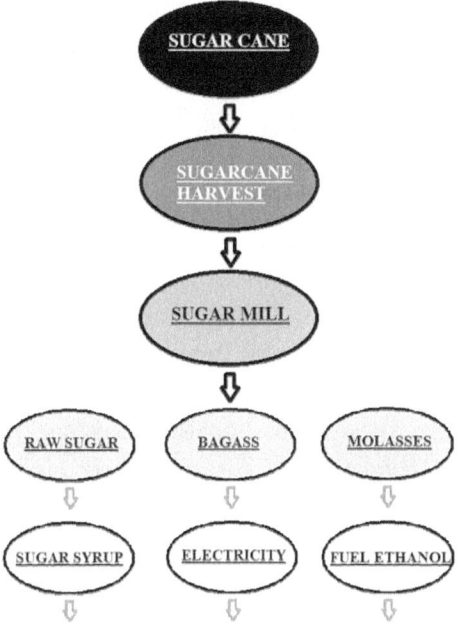

Now the process results in by-products like the following:

1. Bagasse
   a. It can be used as a fuel by burning it, which results in the effective cost of producing sugar in the season.
   b. It can be sold to ply makers who make MDF boards that are used to make good, light, and strong furniture.

2. Molasses
   It all goes to the distilling process to produce pure alcohol, which is used in liquor and ethanol to blend with gasoline. A huge market of molasses is in existence, but as of today, it can be traded in only physical form at future markets for it does not exist.

## Summarization

Sugar production clearly determines the highs and lows of molasses, and a stock picker of distillery or brewing companies can predict the cost and earnings situation seeing the sugar movements.

In this book, I am making the point that the commodity by itself is just the tip of the iceberg. It has many facets to it, as many uses are there which determines its value. Also, it has various by-products that add further importance to it, and a speculator should take advantage of all to make a fortune every time he focuses on one.

Even a simple decision of buying new furniture can, to some extent, be determined from the sugar production. As with higher production, more bagasse availability can lead to lower MDF pricing, thus reducing the manufacturing costs and lower prices for the buyer.

In a reverse situation, it can be postponed to some extent till the situation comes in favor.

# Chapter 12

# Gold

The yellow precious metal has been called by various names over the decades, from "an ancient relic" to a "safe haven investment." It is certainly a metal which has attracted the pharaohs of Ancient Egypt to the Incas of modern Peru to the kings all over the world to common man. It emanates obsession. And for me it is just a commodity that one has to speculate and make money.

There are many books written on gold in the past, and many will come out in future talking about the history of gold and how it is a beater of inflation. So we are not going to bank on the same concept; rather, we as usual will stick to the economic principles to arrive at valuing and pricing gold in order to profit from it.

## World's Largest Gold Producers

| COUNTRY | MINE PRODUCTION METRIC TONS |
|---------|------------------------------|
| China | 420 |
| Australia | 330 |
| Russia | 310 |
| USA | 200 |
| Canada | 180 |

(Source: "Largest Producers of Gold by Country, Top Gold Miners, INN," Investingnews.com)

## World's Largest Gold Consumers

| COUNTRY | METRIC TONS |
|---------|-------------|
| China | 984 |
| India | 849 |
| USA | 193 |
| Germany | 124 |
| Thailand | 90 |

(Source: "World Gold Production and Consumption by Country—Top 10," Providentmetals.com)

If we talk about the demand trend of gold in 2020, then more than 48 percent demand comes from investments, 38 percent comes from jewelry, 10 percent comes from central banks, and 4 percent from technology (Source: World Gold Council).

And where supply is concerned as per 2020 World Gold Council statistics, more than 74 percent gold supply comes from mine production and around 23 percent from recycled gold (Source: World Gold Council).

Though all economies need to have some backing of gold to stabilize or control volatility of the currency, for us, some reading of Bretton Woods's agreement and the Washington agreement is a good base to commence.

## The Bretton Woods Agreement, 1944

The Bretton Woods Agreement was negotiated in July 1944 by delegates from forty-four countries at the United Nations Monetary and Financial Conference held in Bretton Woods, New Hampshire. Under this system, gold formed the basis for the US dollar, and other currencies were pegged to the US dollar's value. The Bretton Woods System effectively came to an end in the early 1970s when President Richard M. Nixon announced that the United States would no longer exchange gold for US currency. It also created two important organizations, IMF (International Monetary Fund) and World Bank, which still survive today even after the system ended, and they both act as exchange of international currencies. The system created a currency peg to the US dollar, which was in turn pegged to the price of gold. It hence provided currency stabilization as the countries were required to maintain their currency peg by buying or selling US dollars, therefore reducing exchange rate volatility and fine-tune international trades. But in 1971, concerns dawned that the US gold supply wouldn't be sufficient to cover the number of dollars in circulation, and hence, President Nixon devalued the US dollars relative to the gold prices, later declaring temporary suspension of gold convertibility and eventually the collapse of the system in 1973. Post collapse, countries were free to choose any another country's currency, basket of currencies, or freely float it and let the markets determine its value.

## The Washington Agreement, 1999, 2004 (Second Version), 2009 (Extension)

Under this agreement, the European Central Bank (ECB), eleven central banks of nations in the new European currency, plus those of Sweden, Switzerland, and the United Kingdom, agreed that gold should remain an important element of global monetary reserves and to *limit their sales* to no more than four hundred tons annually over five years. The agreement came in response to concerns in the gold market after the United Kingdom proposed *to sell 58 percent of UK's gold reserve* through bank auctions along with the Swiss National Bank, Austria, Netherlands, and the IMF. This greatly unsettled the markets. Hence, the agreement was a deterrent on putting a cap on European sales.

A second version was signed in 2004, where the Bank of England did not participate. The quantity was revised to five hundred tons annually over five years. In 2009, nineteen banks extended the agreement and committed to not selling more than four hundred tons till 2014, but the IMF did not participate in the agreement. In 2019, the signatory banks agreed not to renew the agreement again, as no large amounts of gold were sold, which actually declined to nearly zero in 2012 and has remained low thereafter.

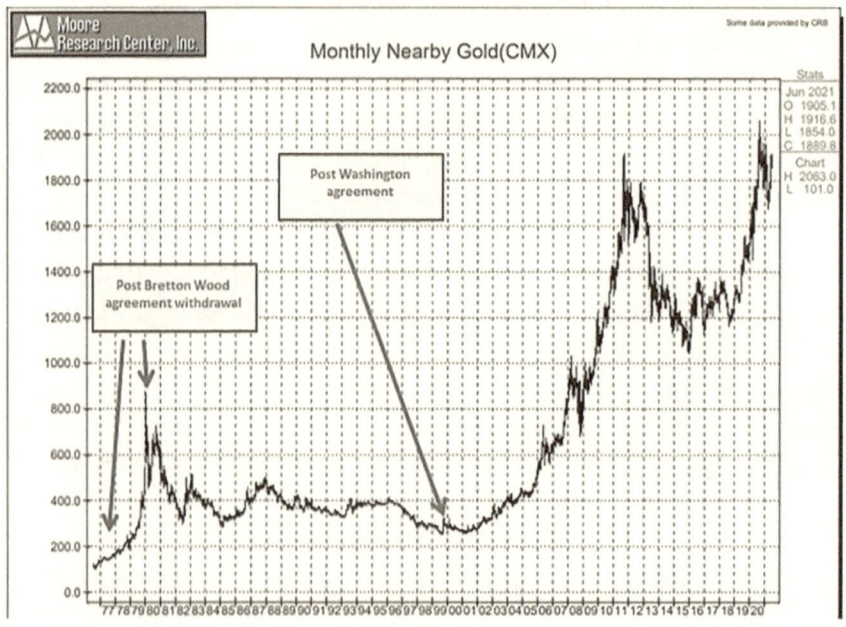

Hence, it makes it clear that commitment was not kept by the United States so it resulted in forced accumulation by the Fed of gold from the early nineties, and the big spurt came in resulting in the strengthening of US dollars vis-à-vis other currency, which again led to further buying by other economies racing gold prices further till all found, more or less, the value at some point uncomfortable to keep procuring gold.

There was trouble in the EU constituents and the use of Washington agreement quotas to sell their five hundred tons per annum to stabilize Euro.

The above has to be kept in the back of one's mind to calculate the sudden additional purchase and rises coming.

# Myths That Need to Be Clarified to Become a Successful Speculator

It has been spoken by experts time and again that as stocks rise, gold falls, and as stocks fall, the investors rush to safe havens and gold rises.

It proves here in these charts how wrong that is.

But once these events occur in reality or the likelihood of such an event not happening increases, gold prices fall.

Note this—during the certainty of events, gold retracts; only till uncertainty brews can gold keep its shiny head rising.

*Indians and Chinese are obsessed with gold.*

Though many view gold as safe haven investments, gold jewelry remains a very important part of a country's culture.

Gold consumption for jewelry by India and China far outweigh that of any other country. They account for 57 percent of global jewelry demand.

The jewelry demand for gold in certain countries is driven by traditions. In India, any marriage is incomplete without the exchange and purchase of gold jewelry. On an average, eight to nine million weddings take place annually.

Below are the world's top jewelry-consuming countries:

Gold Jewelry Consumption Q4 2019

| Rank | Country | Tonnes |
|---|---|---|
| 1 | India | 136.6 |
| 2 | China | 132.1 |
| 3 | U.S. | 34.8 |
| 4 | UAE | 11.5 |
| 5 | Indonesia | 10.7 |
| 6 | United Kingdom | 10.3 |
| 7 | Russia | 9.1 |
| 8 | South Korea | 8.8 |
| 9 | Iran | 8.2 |
| 10 | Italy | 8.1 |

*Source: GFMS Gold Survey 2019 H2 Update & Outlook*

Between 2009 and 2015, China's jewelry market has grown at an incredibly high rate, which eventually stabilized at a growth rate of about 6 percent from 2016.

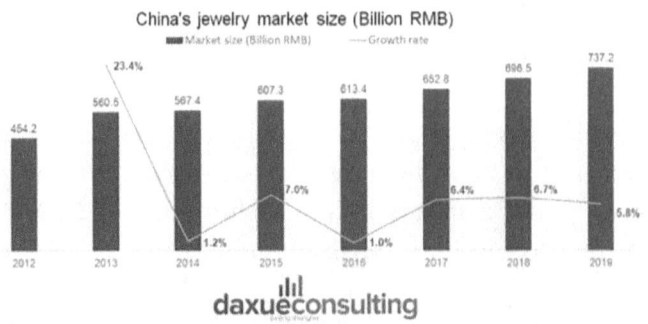

Tier 1 and tier 2 cities are now maturing with their demand. The jewelry demand in tier 3 and tier 4 cities in China is now expanding.

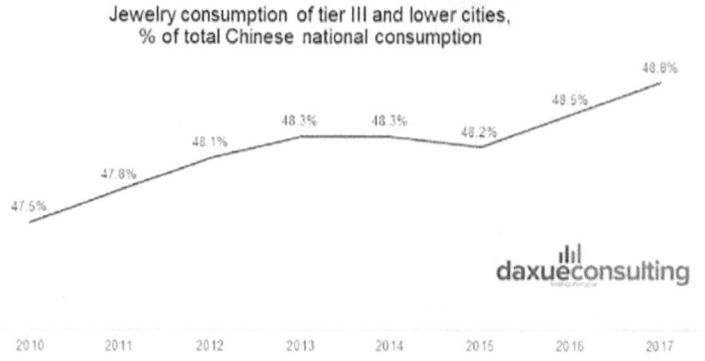

Jewelry consumption of tier III and lower cities, % of total Chinese national consumption

Drivers of purchasing jewelry in China, % (2017)

But as time has gone by and as gold bonds are being issued by the central banks to stop this craze, one has realized that the gold in possession of public is mostly in jewelry form and of 16 Karats on average much lower in purity than presumed. So even if all gold is collected from, say, the Indians (unethical holdings are 24,000 tons, they will be 16 karats, and the value of holdings will not be as astronomical as calculated).

When recession strikes, usually gold is the last asset to collapse, the reason being one needs money to survive the economy and falling incomes, and except gold that is in the savings, what else can be sold when other assets have already lost value?

# Linking Gold to Gold Mining Companies and Jewelry Companies

There is a direct benefit to using prices, provided the gold miners have de-hedged themselves, otherwise, it will be like Ashanti Goldfields Corporation, a gold mining company in 1999, which suffered from an ill-executed gold price hedge, which drove it to the brink of bankruptcy.

Its cash reserves got decimated paying mark to market margins. Hence, reading of financials becomes crucial to know what the gold miners are strategizing and their approach.

Gold miners make a lot of money when gold prices are moderately high and very stable.

The cost of gold extraction and the incremental mining cost as one goes deeper needs to be worked out.

Let us see the top gold mining companies.

| TOP 3 COMPANIES | GOLD PRODUCTION MOz |
|---|---|
| | 2020 |
| Newmont Gold Corp. | 5.91 |
| Barrick Gold Corp. | 4.79 |
| Anglogold Ashanti | 3.05W |

(Courtesy of "Top 10 Gold Mining Companies," Kitco.com)

Newmont Goldcorp Monthly Chart

*Courtesy of www.investing.com.*

## Barrick Gold Corp Monthly Chart

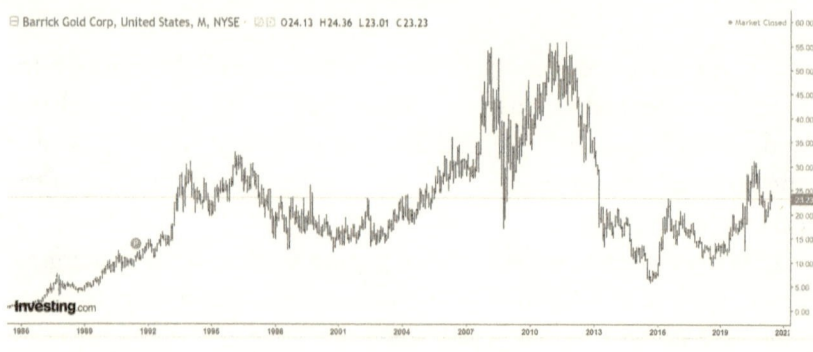

(Courtesy of www.investing.com)

## Anglogold Ashanti Monthly Chart

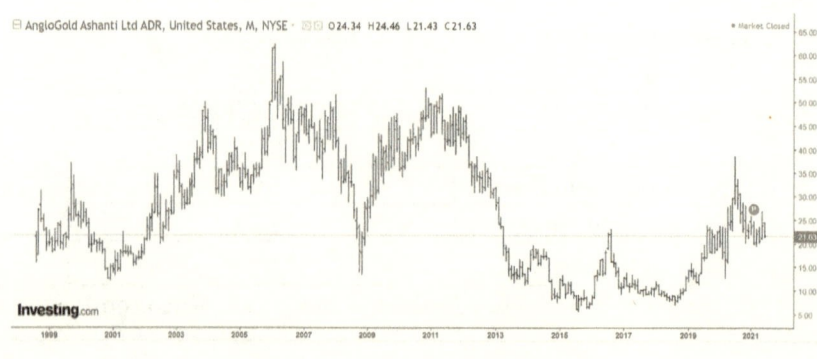

(Courtesy of www.investing.com)

Let us see the jewelry companies like Signet and Pandora, which benefit when gold prices fall.

## Signet Monthly Chart

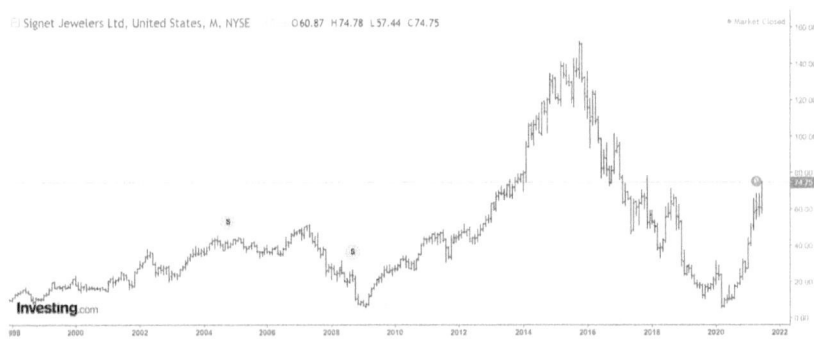

(Courtesy of www.investing.com)

The reason is very evident that these companies can accumulate gold at a lower price but still keep their profit margins on the basis of higher gold prices. So again, just on the basis of a simple price trend, one can decipher that the company will benefit. Post which one can go into the deeper financials and number crunching to arrive at more accurate earnings forecast and thus the eventual price targets.

## Pandora Monthly Chart

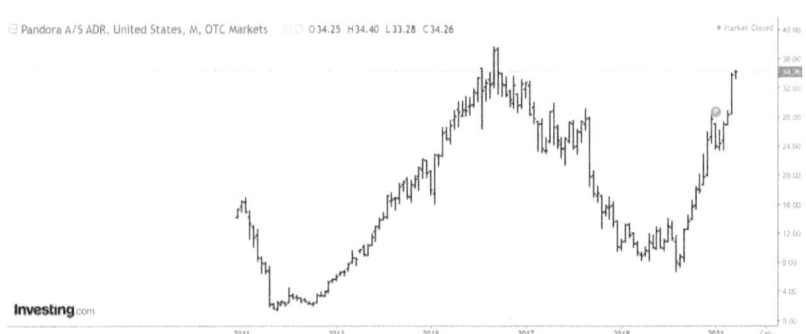

(Courtesy of www.investing.com)

# Chapter 13

## Silver

Silver is called the poor cousin of gold; however, it tends to be more volatile than gold. Its uses make it a precious metal as well as an industrial metal. And one, to make money from it, needs to understand what role it is playing currently and what it will play in the times to come.

### World's Top Silver-Producing Countries

| RANKING | COUNTRY | METRIC TONS |
|---|---|---|
| 1 | Mexico | 6,300 |
| 2 | Peru | 3,800 |
| 3 | China | 3,600 |
| 4 | Russia | 2,100 |
| 5 | Poland | 1,700 |
| 6 | Australia | 1,400 |
| 7 | Chile | 1,300 |
| 8 | Bolivia | 1,200 |
| 9 | Argentina | 1,200 |
| 10 | United States | 980 |

(Source: "Top Silver-Producing Countries,
Mexico Is in the Lead," INN [investingnews.com])

# World's Silver Supply and Demand

Silver Supply and Demand

| Million ounces | 2012 | 2013 | 2014 | 2015 | 2016 | 2017 | 2018 | 2019 | 2020 | 2021F | Year on Year 2020 | 2021 |
|---|---|---|---|---|---|---|---|---|---|---|---|---|
| **Supply** | | | | | | | | | | | | |
| Mine Production | 795.9 | 845.3 | 881.9 | 896.4 | 899.4 | 862.9 | 848.4 | 833.2 | 784.4 | 848.5 | -6% | 8% |
| Recycling | 216.0 | 192.7 | 175.0 | 166.5 | 164.5 | 167.8 | 167.8 | 170.5 | 182.1 | 196.2 | 7% | 8% |
| Net Hedging Supply | | | 10.7 | 2.2 | | | | 13.9 | 8.5 | 10.0 | -39% | 18% |
| Net Official Sector Sales | 3.6 | 1.7 | 1.2 | 1.1 | 1.1 | 1.0 | 1.2 | 1.0 | 1.2 | 1.5 | 18% | 27% |
| Total Supply | 1,015.5 | 1,039.8 | 1,068.7 | 1,066.2 | 1,065.0 | 1,031.7 | 1,017.3 | 1,018.7 | 976.2 | 1,056.3 | -4% | 8% |
| **Demand** | | | | | | | | | | | | |
| Industrial | 460.5 | 460.8 | 456.0 | 457.0 | 491.5 | 518.7 | 513.4 | 514.6 | 486.8 | 524.0 | -3% | 8% |
| of which photovoltaics | 55.0 | 50.5 | 48.4 | 54.1 | 93.7 | 101.8 | 92.5 | 98.7 | 101.0 | 105.0 | 2% | 4% |
| Photography | 92.5 | 45.8 | 43.6 | 41.2 | 37.8 | 38.1 | 33.8 | 32.7 | 27.6 | 28.8 | -16% | 4% |
| Jewelry | 159.0 | 186.9 | 192.8 | 201.6 | 188.4 | 195.3 | 202.0 | 200.3 | 148.6 | 184.4 | -26% | 24% |
| Silverware | 40.7 | 46.5 | 53.6 | 57.9 | 53.9 | 59.6 | 67.6 | 62.1 | 32.6 | 43.1 | -48% | 32% |
| Net Physical Investment | 241.9 | 301.9 | 284.6 | 312.6 | 213.6 | 156.2 | 165.6 | 185.7 | 200.5 | 252.8 | 8% | 26% |
| Net Hedging Demand | 40.4 | 29.3 | | | 12.0 | 1.1 | 7.4 | | | | na | na |
| Total Demand | 985.1 | 1,071.2 | 1,024.6 | 1,070.4 | 997.2 | 968.0 | 989.8 | 995.4 | 896.1 | 1,033.0 | -10% | 15% |
| Market Balance | 30.5 | 31.5 | 44.1 | 4.2 | 67.8 | 65.7 | 27.6 | 23.3 | 80.1 | 23.3 | 244% | -71% |
| Net Investment in ETPs | 53.6 | 4.7 | -0.3 | -17.1 | 53.9 | 7.2 | 21.4 | 83.3 | 331.1 | 150.0 | 298% | -55% |
| Market Balance less ETPs | -23.2 | 36.2 | 44.3 | 12.9 | 13.9 | 58.5 | 49.0 | -60.0 | -251.0 | 126.7 | 319% | -50% |
| Silver Price (US$/oz, London price) | 31.2 | 23.8 | 19.1 | 15.7 | 17.1 | 17.1 | 15.7 | 16.2 | 20.6 | 27.3 | 27% | 33% |

Source: Metals Focus

Material and statistics in this section were adapted in part from the Silver Institute's *World Silver Survey 2021*.

Silver has created and destroyed more millionaires than any other commodity. One stark profile is of the Hunt Brothers. Silver is not just poor man's gold and treated as a precious metal but also has numerous uses, and prices of silver companies fluctuate depending on industry demand for silver.

## Silver Monthly Chart

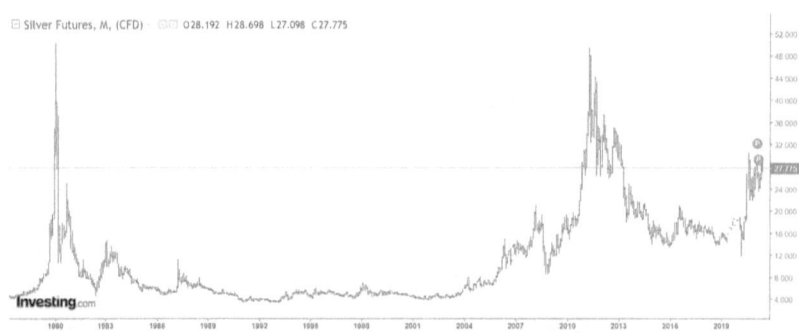

(Courtesy of www.investing.com)

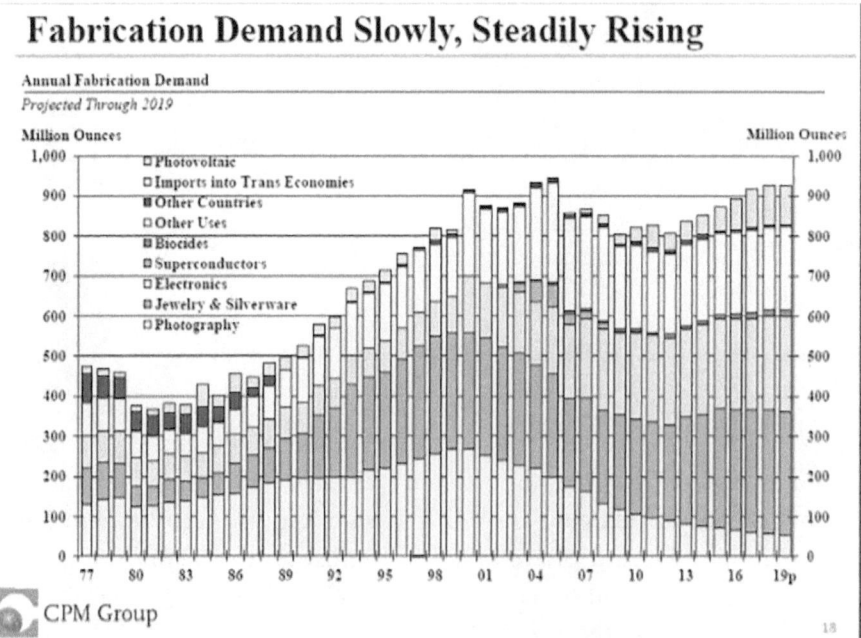

(Source: CPM Group Report)

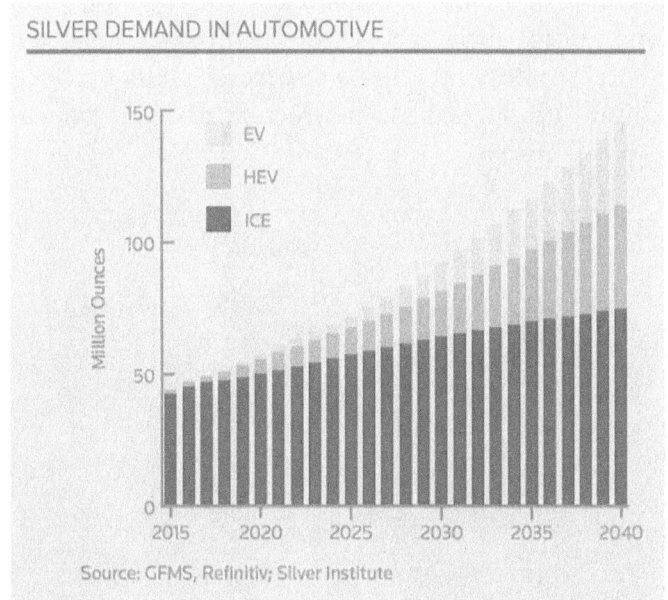

Source: The Silver Institute

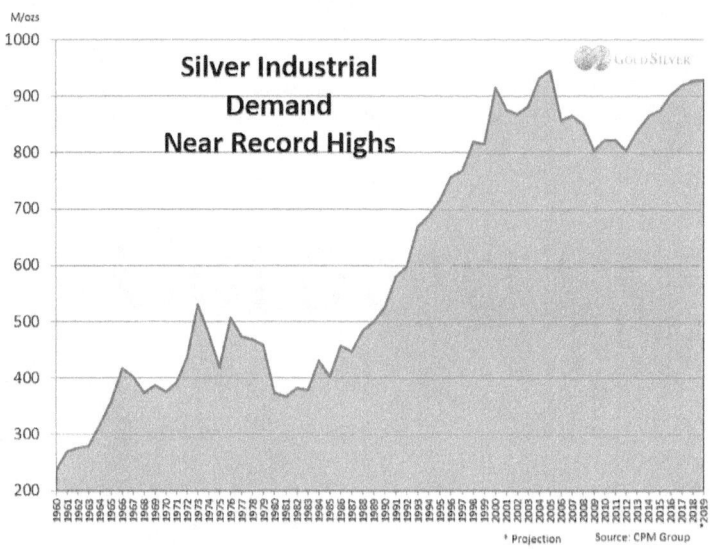

With growth of solar farms as one of the most important shifts from conventional fossil fuel to the new conventional renewable energy source, its demand is likely to become pretty much constant, which will fill up the demand destruction that was created by the photography industry.

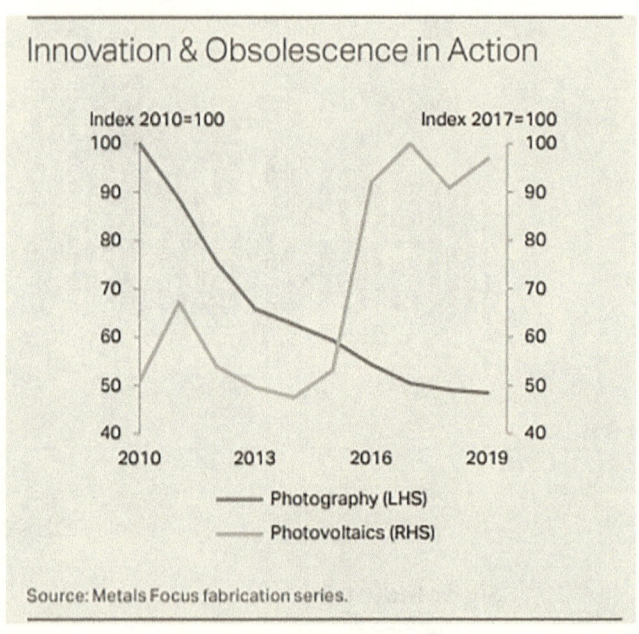

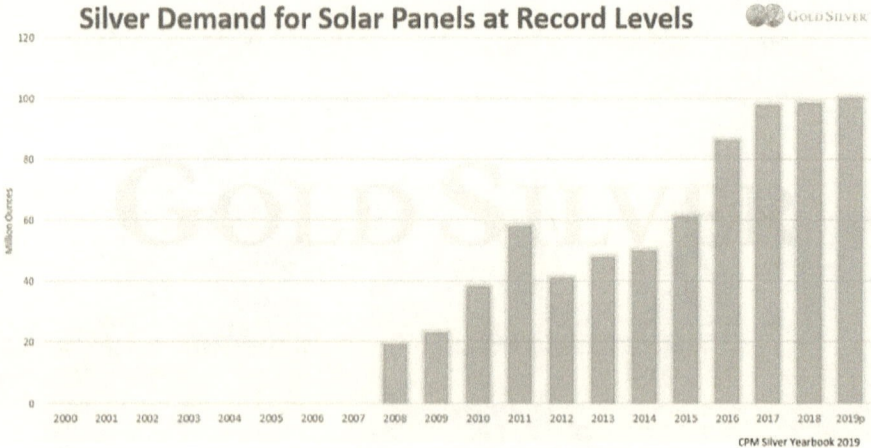

## Uses of Silver

1. Uses of silver in medicine and healthcare
   - Silver sulfadiazine used as a topical cream to treat burns.
   - Treatment of warts and corns usually in the form of a caustic pencil.
   - SilverCoat Foley catheters are used in urology.
   - Radiology.
   - Bandages and dressings.
   - Surgical mesh.
   - Conjunctivitis.
   - Prevent cavities and dental fillings.
   - Silver needles and sutures.
   - Silver bearing coatings for hip joint implants named as SMART-HIP.
   - NASA utilized silver ions as a lightweight water purifier for the Apollo spacecraft.
   - Water purification.
   - Antimicrobial lab coats.
   - Cauterizing agent for stomas or openings in surgery.
   - Silver nano wire biosensors.
   - Surface disinfectant.
   - Surgical masks.
2. Uses of silver in electronics and technology
   - Circuit board contacts
   - Speaker wires
   - Railway switch gear
   - Superconductors
   - Media storage
3. Uses of silver in energy and science
   - Solar panels.
   - Silver oxide and silver zinc batteries
   - Thermal and infrared telescopes
   - Control rods in nuclear reactors
   - Silver acts as a catalyst

- Explosives
- Silver iodide is often used for weather modification or cloud seeding
- 3D printing
- Semiconductors
- Uses of silver in the home
- Photography
- Use in mirrors
- Jewelry
- Silverware
- Coins and investment
- Food containers
- Washing machines, refrigerators, and air-conditioning
- Car engine bearings

(Source: www.silvercoins.com)

## The World's Top Silver Producers in 2020

| COMPANY | 2020 AG OUTPUT, MOZ |
|---|---|
| Fresnillo | 53.1 |
| KGHM | 43.4 |
| Glencore | 32.8 |
| CODELCO | 27.0 |
| Vedanta (Hindustan zinc) | 23.7 |
| Pan American silver | 17.3 |
| Hecla | 13.5 |

(Source: www.kitco.com)

Not all the above companies are exclusive silver-producing companies; hence charts of only exclusive silver companies are given below to easily understand the price movement.

## Fresnillo Monthly Chart

(Courtesy of www.investing.com)

## Hecla Mining Monthly Chart

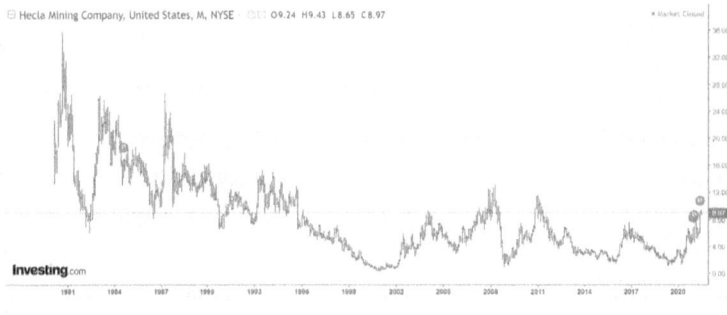

(Courtesy of www.investing.com)

## Pan American Silver Corp Monthly Chart

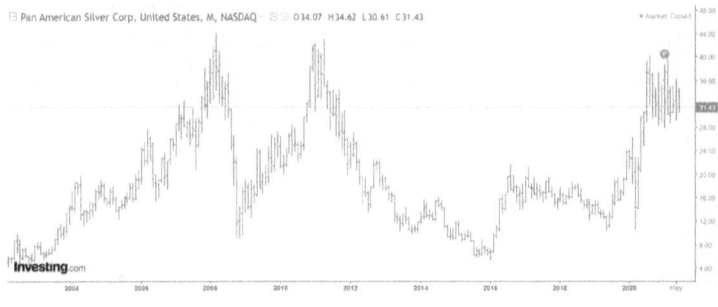

(Courtesy of www.investing.com)

# Chapter 14

## Copper

The king of metals is also called Dr. Copper, as this metal's movement most of the time reveals the state of the economy, and then one can forecast the likely economies of the stock market in the medium-term future.

The reddish-gold metal has a range of industrial uses and is often used in electronics due to its high electrical conductivity and its ability to be easily shaped into wiring. It is also a good conductor of heat, giving it additional properties prized by the industry. Copper plays a big role in the electrification of world's energy system.

### World's Top Copper-Producing Countries in 2020

| RANKING | COUNTRY | MILLION METRIC TONS |
|---------|---------|---------------------|
| 1 | Chile | 5.7 |
| 2 | Peru | 2.2 |
| 3 | China | 1.7 |
| 4 | Congo | 1.3 |
| 5 | United States | 1.2 |

(Source: https://www.nsenergybusiness.com)

## Leading copper ore importing countries worldwide in 2018
*(in billion U.S. dollars)*

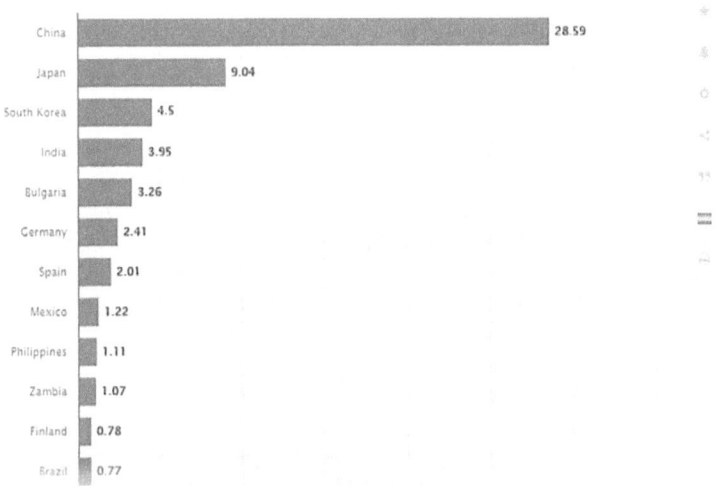

(Source: "Copper Ore Imports Worldwide by Country, 2018," *Statista*)

## Copper Monthly Price Chart

(Courtesy of www.investing.com)

So if prices of copper go higher, certainly the cost of inputs of wire manufacturing companies or pipeline companies in infrastructure companies will be on an upswing and so in the opposite direction.

In my view, one of the greatest demands for destruction for the metal is the loss of the last mile of the copper wires as wireless tech gains more momentum, and this gap can only be filled by the EV revolution globally as statistics reveal the usage of copper for such vehicles is set to rise 250 percent by 2030.

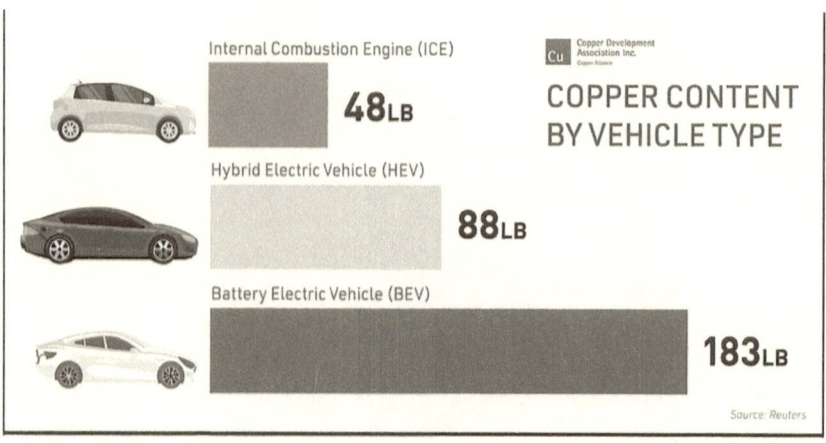

And in the future, the substitutes and alternative metals too need to be seen with the rise and fall in pricing of copper. This will be common to all metals and most commodities as none can have completed inelastic demand vis-à-vis its pricing.

## Top Copper-Producing Companies in 2020

| COMPANY | PRODUCTION IN MILLION TONS |
|---|---|
| CODELCO | 1.73 |
| BHP Group | 1.72 |
| Freeport-McMoran | 1.45 |
| Glencore | 1.26 |
| Southern Copper | 1 |

(Source: https://www.nsenergybusiness.com)

## Bhp Billiton Limited ADR Monthly Chart

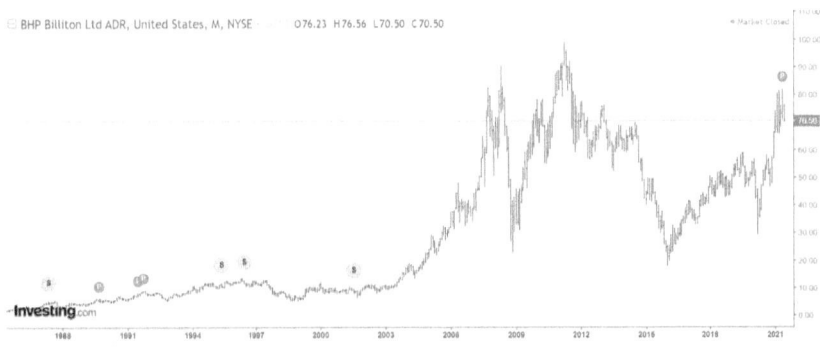

(Courtesy of www.investing.com)

## Freeport-McMoran Monthly Chart

(Courtesy of www.investing.com)

## Southern Copper Monthly Chart

(Courtesy of www.investing.com)

Note: Our base research revealed we are not going into the primary and secondary sources of producing copper and its effects, as we are going to stick to the metal, its pricing, and its effect on stocks.

# Chapter 15

## Aluminum

Aluminum is almost always alloyed, which improves its mechanical properties, especially when tempered. The main alloying agents are copper, zinc, magnesium, manganese, and silicon aluminum, both wrought and cast, which has been alloyed with manganese, silicon, magnesium, copper, and zinc among others. Aluminum has very low density, is easily fabricated, durable, cheap, has adequate mechanical strength, is nontoxic, non-absorptive, and resists corrosion. Aluminum can be recycled, and clean aluminum has residual market value.

The major uses for aluminum metal by industry are the following:

- **Transportation, 27%**—automobiles, aircraft, trucks, railway cars, marine vessels, bicycles, spacecraft
- **Building and construction, 25%**—windows, doors, siding, building wire, sheathing, roofing
- **Packaging, 16%**—cans, foil, frame
- **Electricity-related uses, 13%**—conductor alloys, motors, and generators, transformers, capacitors
- **Machinery and equipment, 9%**—processing equipment, pipes, tools
- **Consumer goods, household items, and others, 10%**—cooking utensils, furniture

## World's Top Aluminum-Producing Countries in 2020

| RANKING | COUNTRY | MILLION METRIC TONS |
|---------|---------|---------------------|
| 1 | China | 37 |
| 2 | Russia | 3.6 |
| 3 | India | 3.6 |
| 4 | Canada | 3.1 |
| 5 | United Arab Emirates | 2.6 |

(Source: www.statista.com)

## The Raw Material Ratio

The greatest cost element in aluminum extraction is power. It is said that 63 percent of its cost element is electricity charges. Hence, extraction cost as well as the extracting company's ability on cost control eventually affects the price of aluminum and its demand.

How is aluminum produced?

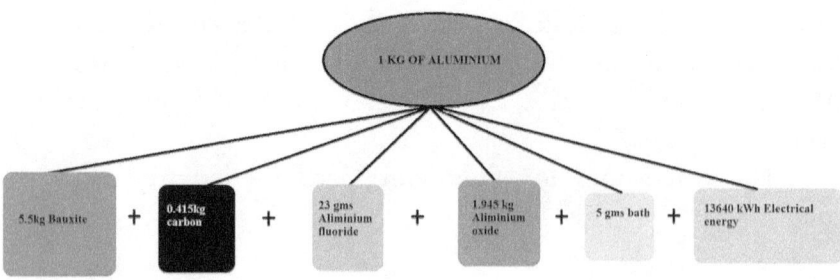

List of Countries by Bauxite Production in 2020

| RANKING | COUNTRY | PRODUCTION (THOUSAND TONNES) |
|---------|---------|------------------------------|
| 1 | Australia | 86,400 |
| 2 | China | 79,000 |
| 3 | Guinea | 57,000 |
| 4 | Brazil | 29,000 |
| 5 | India | 23,000 |

(Source: www.wikipedia.com)

## Top Aluminum Companies in the World, 2020

| COMPANY | PRODUCTION CAPACITY (million tons) |
|---------|------------------------------------|
| Hongqiao | 5.7 |
| Rusal | 3.8 |
| Rio Tinto Alcan | 3.2 |
| Alcoa | 2.3 |

(Source: www.statista.com)

## Aluminum Monthly Price Chart

(Courtesy: www.investing.com)

## Hongqiao Monthly Chart

(Courtesy of www.investing.com)

## Rusal Monthly Chart

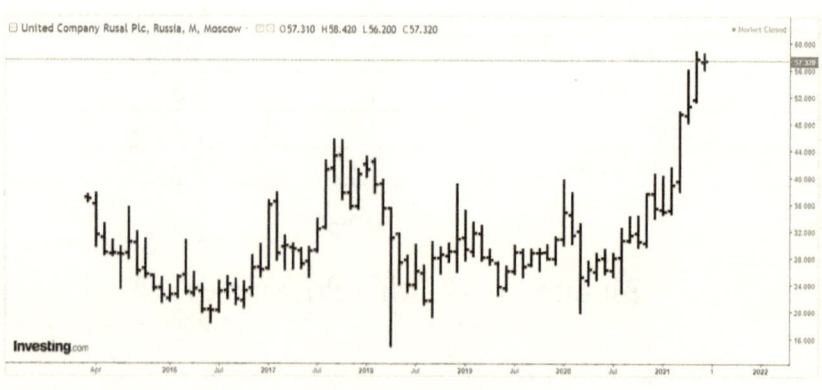

(Courtesy of www.investing.com)

## Rio Tinto Monthly Chart

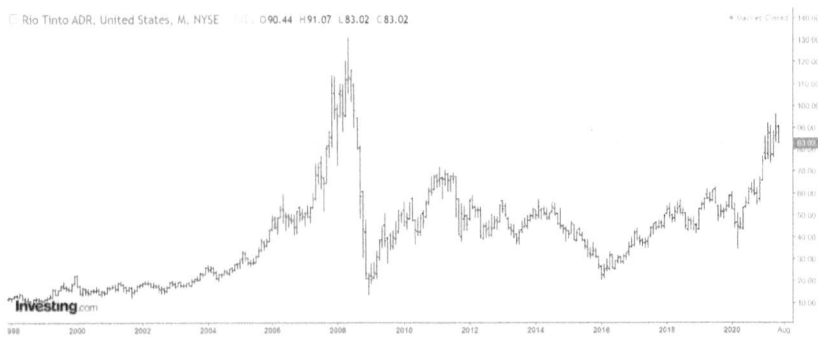

(Courtesy of www.investing.com)

## Alcoa Monthly Chart

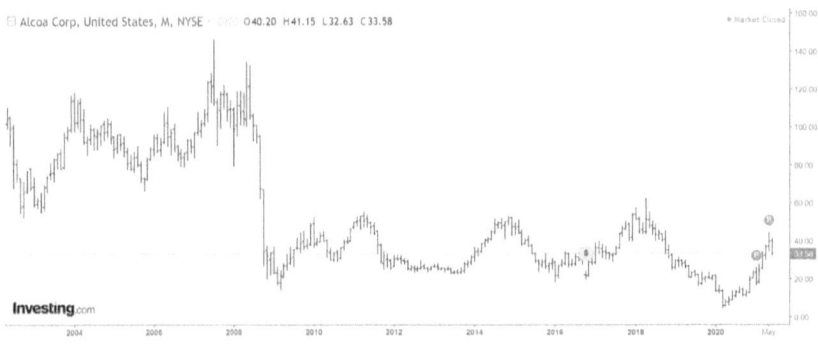

(Courtesy of www.investing.com)

## Summarization

As aluminum moves, with a minor time lag, the companies also start their trajectory in the same lines, keeping all other company specific fundamentals and financials aside. One needs to decide whether one wants to take advantage from the commodity aspect of trading first (which needs deeper pockets to withstand high volatility and margin calls) or to directly invest in the companies and take advantage of that.

Otherwise, futures and options are also available in most stocks in case a person wants to stick with stocks and avoid the commodity. However, understanding the commodity is very crucial in order to have the first mover advantage whether from investing or dis-investing or buying/selling futures and options or even shorting.

In the coming chapters on zinc, nickel, lead, and steel the above point again gains clarity. Hence, I am avoiding repetitions of that nature. The description and the pictorial presentation itself will make your mind convinced...

# Chapter 16

## Zinc

Zinc is a very strategic metal indeed.

Zinc is a corrosion-resistant zinc plating of iron. It is a fair conductor of electricity. Its greatest use is in production of galvanized steel—the steel that can be molded but keeps its strength. For example, huge bridges across sea and river coastal connectors. This contributes to 50 percent of total zinc demand.

Other applications are in electrical batteries, small non-structural castings, and die casting, which contributes to 17 percent of zinc usage, and alloys such as brass, which contributes to 17 percent of zinc demand. It also uses defense equipment like armored vehicles and even robots. So it has a very futuristic market by itself.

Hence, again, it is an infrastructure metal.

### World's Top Zinc-Producing Countries in 2019

| RANK | COUNTRY | PRODUCTION (TONNES) |
|---|---|---|
| 1 | China | 4,300,000 |
| 2 | Peru | 1,400,000 |
| 3 | Australia | 1,300,000 |
| 4 | India | 800,000 |
| 5 | United States | 780,000 |

(Source: *Wikipedia*)

Let us see the price movement of zinc companies vis-à-vis zinc prices.

## Zinc Monthly Price Chart

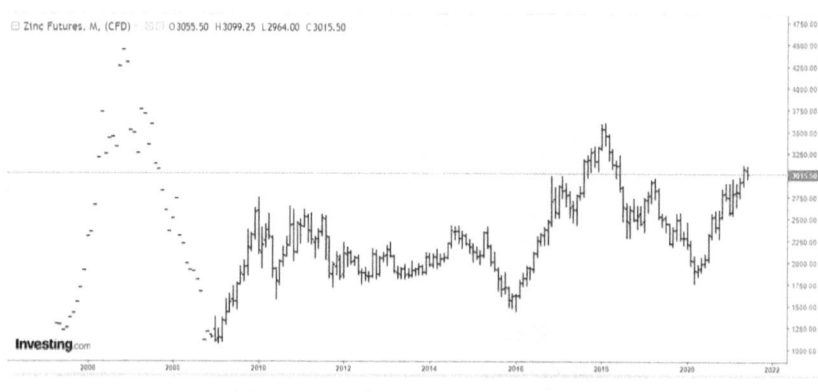

(Courtesy of www.investing.com)

## Teck Resources Monthly Price Chart

(Courtesy of www.investing.com)

## Hudbay Mineral Monthly Price Chart

(Courtesy of www.investing.com)

# Chapter 17

## Nickel

Nickel is used in many industrial and consumer products, including stainless steel, alnico magnets, coinage, rechargeable batteries, electric guitar strings, microphone capsules, and plating on plumbing fixtures. Nickel is preeminently an alloy metal, and its chief use is in nickel steels and nickel cast irons, in which it typically increases the tensile strength, toughness, and elastic limit. It is widely used in many other alloys, including nickel brasses and bronzes and alloys with many other metals.

Nickel and its alloys are frequently used as catalysts for hydrogenation reactions.

Nickel is a naturally magnetostrictive material, meaning that in the presence of a magnetic field, the material undergoes a small change in length.

# World's Primary Nickel Consumption by Industry in 2019

| USAGE | CONSUMPTION IN THOUSAND METRIC TONS |
|---|---|
| Stainless steel | 1775 |
| Batteries | 175 |
| Special steels | 150 |
| Electroplating | 150 |
| Other | 250 |

(Source: *Bloomberg*)

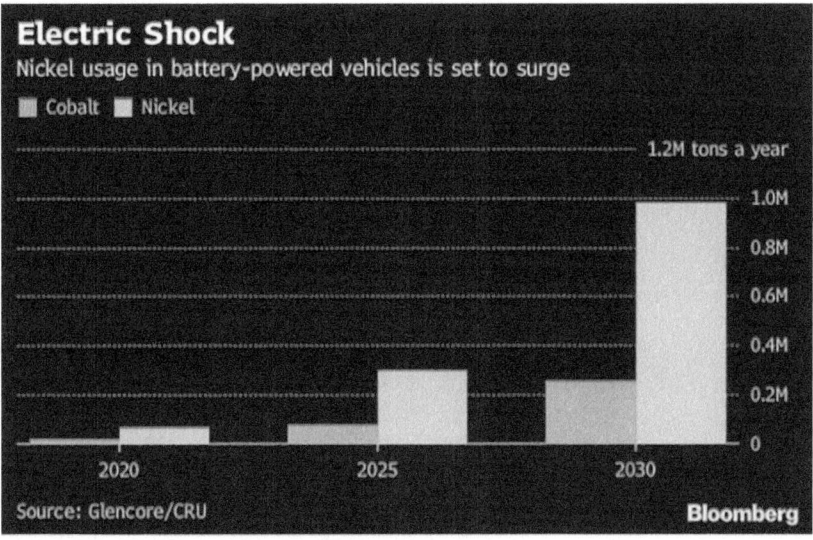

Nickel consumption projections for EVs provided by Bloomberg.

(Source: *Bloomberg*)

Let us see the nickel-producing countries' company prices vis-à-vis the metal prices.

## World's Top Nickel-Producing Countries in 2020

| RANK | COUNTRY | MINE PRODUCTION IN THOUSAND METRIC TONS |
|---|---|---|
| 1 | Indonesia | 760 |
| 2 | Philippines | 320 |
| 3 | Russia | 280 |
| 4 | New Caledonia (France) | 200 |
| 5 | Australia | 170 |
| 6 | Canada | 150 |

(Source: www.statista.com)

Nickel Price Chart Monthly

(Courtesy of www.investing.com)

## Vale Price Chart Monthly

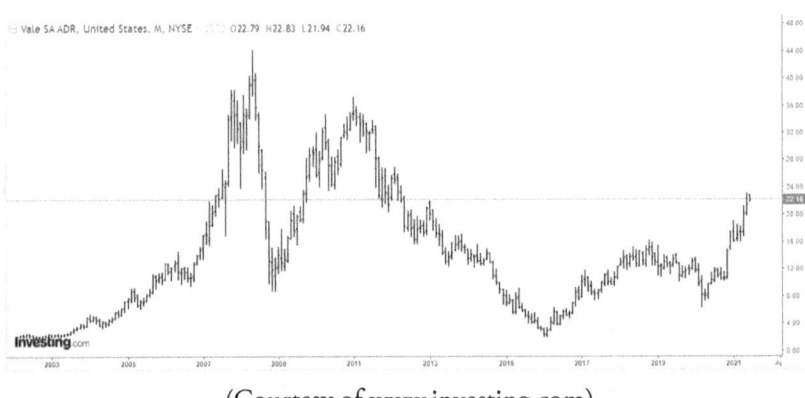

(Courtesy of www.investing.com)

## Norilsk Nickel Price Chart Monthly

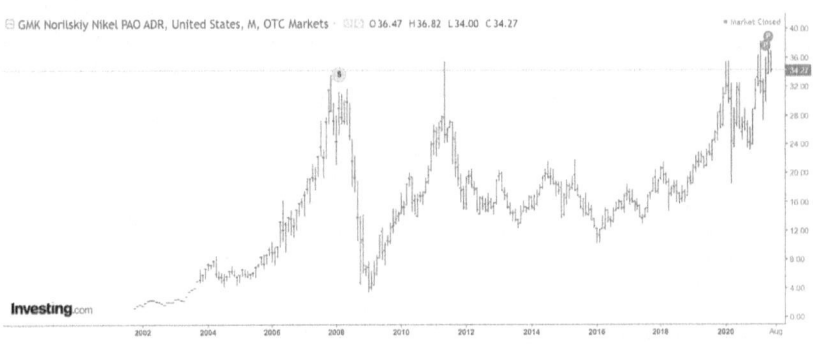

(Courtesy of www.investing.com)

The nickel market is controlled by lot of cartels in Russia, Indonesia, and the Philippines.

## Nickel Asia Corp Price Chart Monthly

(Courtesy of www.investing.com)

# Chapter 18

# Lead

Lead is still widely used for car batteries, which constitutes 74 percent of lead demand; pigments constitute 9 percent rolls; and extruded products constitutes 8 percent of demand and other usages in alloys, ammunition, cable sheathing, weights for lifting, weight belts for diving, lead crystal glass, radiation protection, used in some solders, and used to store corrosive liquids 11 percent demand.

## Top Lead-Producing Countries in 2020

| RANK | COUNTRY | MINE PRODUCTION IN THOUSAND METRIC TONS |
|------|---------|------------------------------------------|
| 1 | China | 1900 |
| 2 | Australia | 480 |
| 3 | United States | 290 |
| 4 | Peru | 240 |
| 5 | Mexico | 240 |
| 6 | Russia | 220 |
| 7 | India | 210 |

Source: https://www.statista.com)

# World's Lead-Producing Companies in 2020

| NAME | MINE PRODUCTION IN THOUSAND METRIC TONS |
|------|------------------------------------------|
| Glencore | 280 |
| Doe Run | 250 |
| Hindustan Zinc | 198 |
| Teck | 103 |

(Source: https://www.statista.com)

## Lead Monthly Price Chart

(Courtesy of www.investing.com)

## Glencore Monthly Chart

(Courtesy of www.investing.com)

# Chapter 19

## Iron and Steel

Major uses of steel are in building and infrastructure 50 percent, mechanical equipment 16 percent, automotive 13 percent, metal products 11 percent, shipping rail 5 percent, and others 5 percent.

### WORLD'S TOP IRON ORE-PRODUCING COUNTRIES IN 2020

| RANKING | COUNTRY | USABLE PRODUCTION IN MILLION METRIC TONS |
|---------|---------|------------------------------------------|
| 1 | Australia | 900 |
| 2 | Brazil | 400 |
| 3 | China | 340 |
| 4 | India | 230 |
| 5 | Russia | 95 |
| 6 | South Africa | 71 |

(Source: https://www.statista.com)

## World's Crude Steel-Producing Countries

| RANKING | COUNTRY | MILLION METRIC TONNES |
|---------|---------|-----------------------|
| 1 | China | 1,053 |
| 2 | India | 99.2 |
| 3 | Japan | 83.2 |
| 4 | Russia | 73.4 |
| 5 | United States | 72.7 |
| 6 | South Korea | 67.1 |

(Source: https://www.statista.com)

## World's Top Largest Iron Ore-Producing Companies in 2020

| RANKING | COMPANY | PRODUCTION IN MILLION TONNES |
|---------|---------|------------------------------|
| 1 | Vale | 300 |
| 2 | Rio Tinto | 286 |
| 3 | BHP | 248 |
| 4 | Fortescue Metals Group | 204 |
| 5 | Anglo American | 61 |

(Source: www.nsenergybusiness.com)

## World's Top Crude Steel Production Companies

| RANKING | COMPANY | PRODUCTION IN MILLION TONNES |
|---------|---------|------------------------------|
| 1 | Arecelor Mittal | 96.42 |
| 2 | China Baowu Group | 67.43 |
| 3 | Nippon Steel Corporation | 49.22 |
| 4 | HBIS Group | 46.80 |
| 5 | POSCO | 42.86 |

(Source: https://www.statista.com)

It is an ageless metal, and its costing becomes very influential from iron ore mine to the steel that may or may not be the final product.

With the fineness of iron ore 63+, costing of iron ore becomes the raw material cost of steel. Just like fossil fuel, iron ore mines also do cause a lot of environmental damage. And that is also a cost we humans have to bear.

## Iron Ore Weekly Price Chart

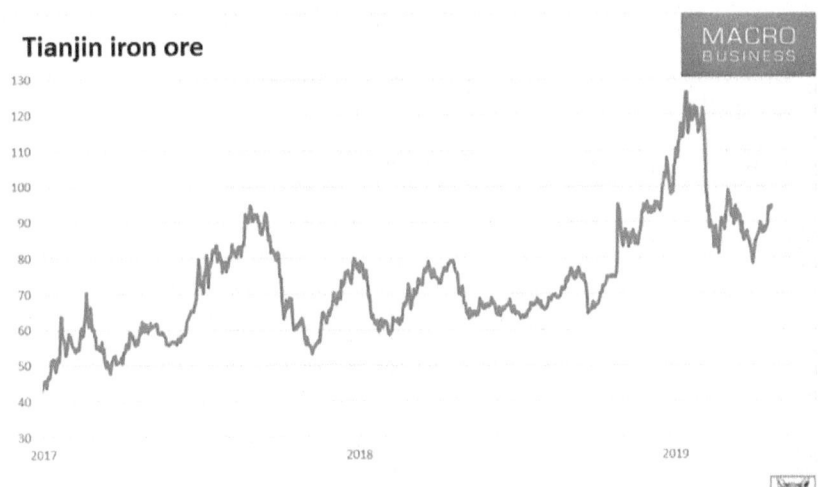

(Courtesy of https://www.statista.com)

## China Monthly Steel Prices

(Courtesy of https://www.statista.com)

## Arcelor Mittal Monthly Price Chart

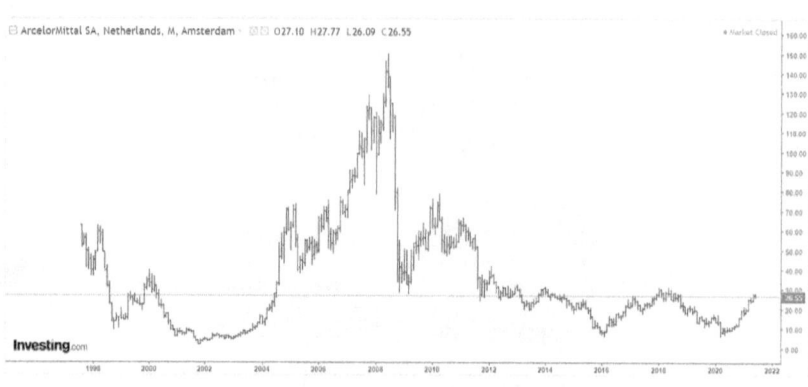

(Courtesy of https://www.statista.com)

## China Baoan Monthly Price Chart

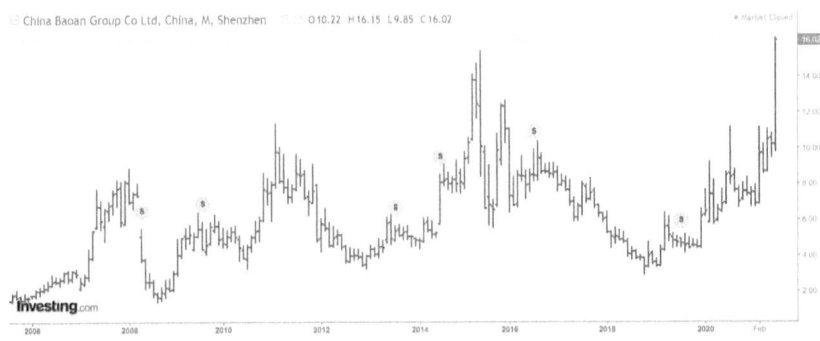

*(Courtesy of https://www.statista.com)*

## POSCO Monthly Price Chart

(Courtesy of https://www.statista.com)

## Nippon Steel Monthly Price Chart

(Courtesy of https://www.statista.com)

# Chapter 20

## Oilseeds and Softs

The two chapters ahead are going to be agro based, and we know from earlier what is needed to analyze the chapter 10, where we will show their graphical impact on the companies and how we benefit from.

### Oilseeds

This is one of the fastest-growing agriculture markets due to its universal application in the food industry, pharmaceutical industry, cosmetics, as well as animal feed industry.

The oil that is extracted from the oilseed is used as food for human consumption and residue or by-product goes toward animal feed.

The major crops in the complex are the following:

- Groundnut
- Sunflower
- Cottonseed
- Rapeseed and canola
- Soybean
- Palm
- Sesame
- Rice-bran oil
- Castor
- Olive

Large areas of cultivation are being put to use specifically for the oilseeds. This is to such an extent that the Brazilian government took a policy decision of cutting down a section of the vast Amazon jungle to increase the area for soybean cultivation even though Brazil is still the largest grower of soybeans.

Though each oilseed has its own benefits, which we are not analyzing here, they are sometimes even competing with each other due to specific price movements affecting them.

Soybean and palm are the biggest competitors, and they have a lot of impact on various industries as well as other vegetable oils.

One also has to keep in mind that oil extracted is used as a feed-stock for bio-diesel production.

These are highly tending markets, and there is always a chain reaction among them, though the proportion of the rise and fall of each may vary.

Soybean Monthly Price Chart

(Courtesy of www.investing.com)

## Soybean Meal Monthly Price Chart

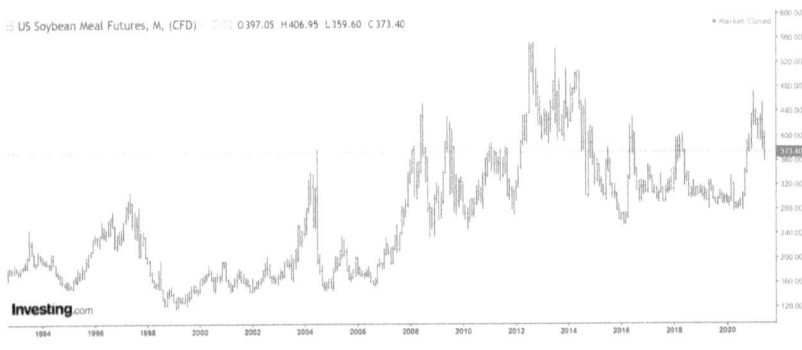

(Courtesy of www.investing.com)

## Archer Daniels Monthly Price Chart

(Courtesy of www.investing.com)

## Bunge Monthly Price Chart

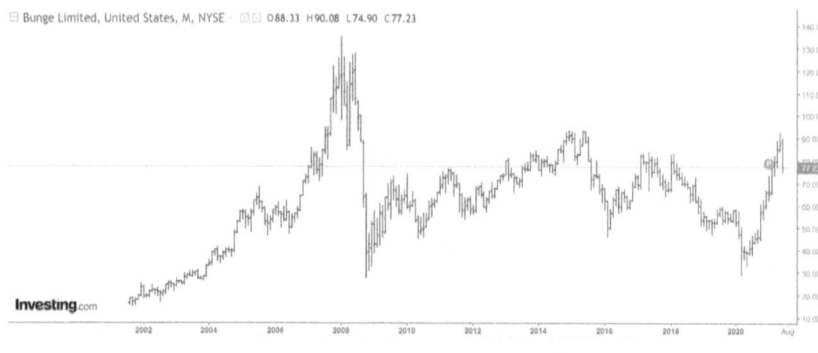

(Courtesy of www.investing.com)

Most soaps/detergents use palm noodles, and this impacts the companies like Unilever's earning margins greatly. Soap noodles are mainly made from palm oil blended with either coconut oil or palm kernel oil.

And these soap noodles eventually result in manufacturing of white soaps and detergent as they are natural and soft on the skin plus biodegradable in nature.

Hence, without even going deep into the financials of certain companies, one can easily decipher and take positions to make enormous profits. As vegetable oil price rise time to dis-invest or short companies like Unilever and vice-versa.

## Palm Oil Monthly Price Chart

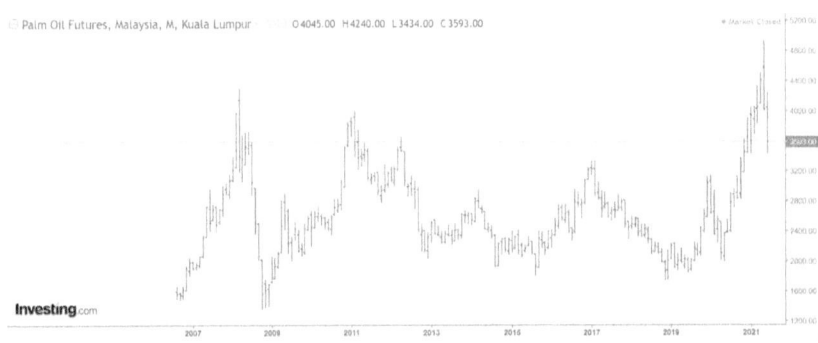

(Courtesy of www.investing.com)

## Unilever Monthly Price Chart

(Courtesy of www.investing.com)

# Softs

As we have already covered sugar as a separate chapter earlier, a few others that impact and are inter-linkable ones I cover in a concise manner here. They are the perishables like cocoa, coffee, cotton, and milk.

# Cocoa

Cocoa was discovered five thousand years ago by the natives of South America and used to be the drink of kings in ancient times. Today, it is grown in a few countries like Cote d' Ivory, Ghana, Ecuador, and Nigeria. It always has a supply issue due to instability of political environment in Africa and hence goes through some real and artificial price volatility. Its price movement directly impacts the changeability of chocolate companies.

Cocoa Monthly Price Chart

(Courtesy of www.investing.com)

Hershey Co. Monthly Price Chart

(Courtesy of www.investing.com)

## Mondelez Monthly Price Chart

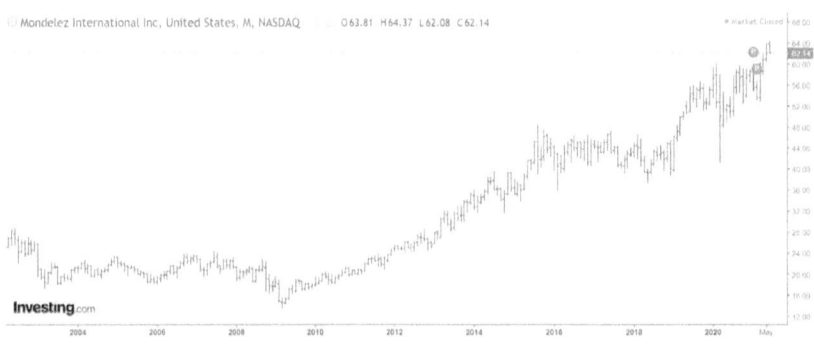

(Courtesy of www.investing.com)

## Summary

All softs will show a very significant inverse ratio with their final product brand companies. The higher their prices, the more the earnings of the companies can affect it, resulting in the fall of the stock prices and vice versa.

## Coffee

Discovered around the ninth century in Ethiopia, it now is the most popular drink among the vast global population.

The different varieties of coffee as well as the blends created have made it so much in demand that its demand many times outstrips supply, thus giving us an opportunity to make money.

## Coffee Monthly Price Chart

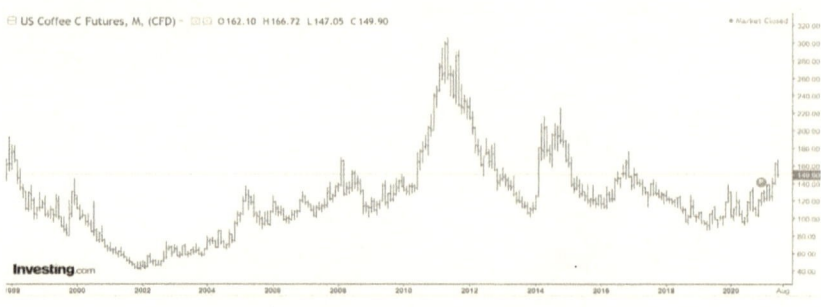

(Courtesy of www.investing.com)

## Starbucks Monthly Price Chart

(Courtesy of www.investing.com)

Now here the relationship is inverse. As coffee prices are lower companies like Starbucks and Dunkin Brands will certainly benefit as coffee is their raw material and the cost of production of their final cup will be lower. Hence, huge profitability will come their way. As soon as coffee prices shoot up, earnings will collapse, leading to good selling opportunities in the stock to earn profit both ways—keeping hold long in coffee's future and selling futures and options in companies like Starbucks.

## Milk

The most perishable of all, this needs no further explanation. All are aware of its use into many products like cheese, butter, cream, ice cream, etc.

### Milk Monthly Price Chart

(Courtesy of www.investing.com)

### Wendy's Monthly Price Chart

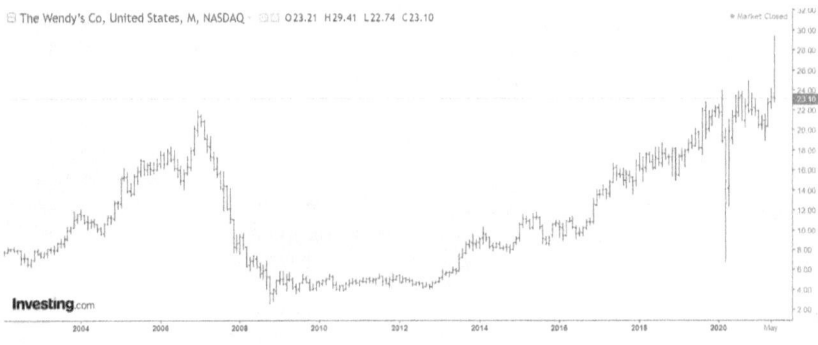

(Courtesy of www.investing.com)

Kraft Heinz Monthly Price Chart

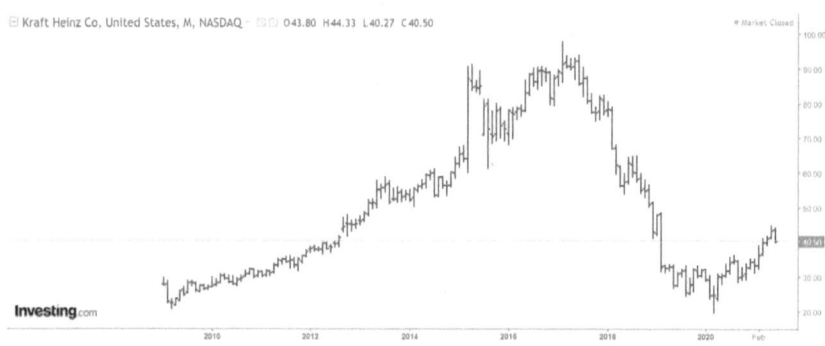

(Courtesy of www.investing.com)

## Cotton

Always referred to as a king of commodities having universal appeal and being the most influential commodity. Let us understand the value chain of seed cotton and its by-product.

Cotton Value Chain

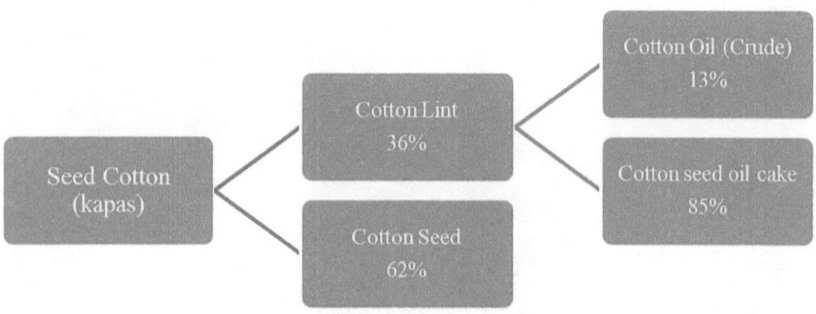

Cotton in the last five centuries has played a vital role in rise and fall of many economies.

Cottonseed oil cake is the best nutrition for cattle in giving high-quality milk.

So this again is a vicious cycle. If crop is low, less cottonseed oil cake is extracted, which results in price rise and less cattle feed, less milk output, and prices of milk rise, eventually impacting earnings and other way around.

## Cotton Monthly Price Chart

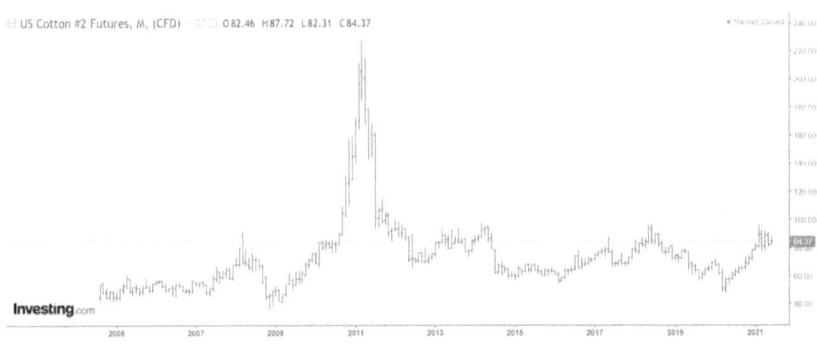

(Courtesy of www.investing.com)

## Cottonseed Oil Cake Monthly Price Chart

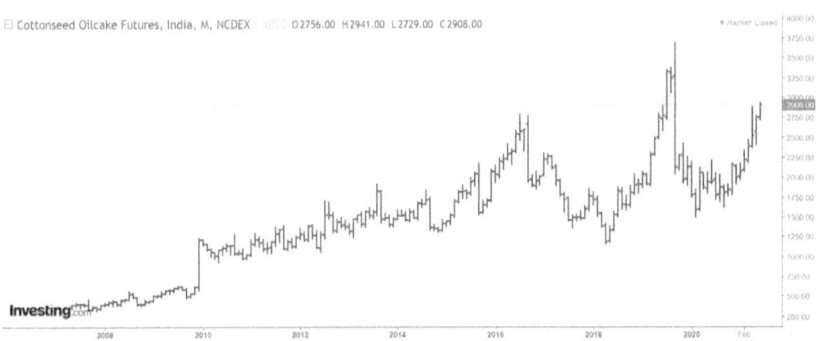

(Courtesy of www.investing.com)

## Carter's Monthly Price Chart

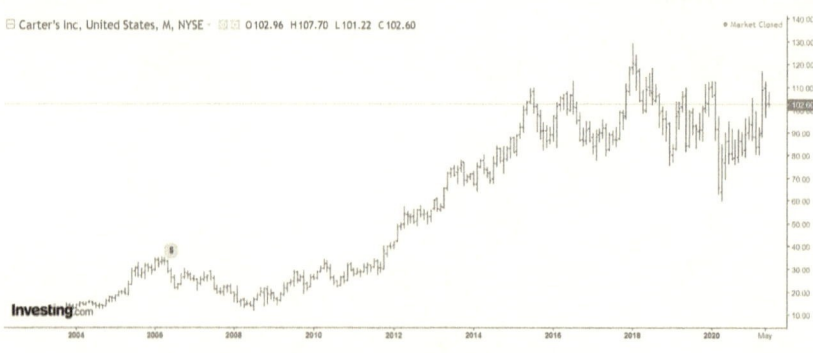

(Courtesy of www.investing.com)

## Gap Monthly Price Chart

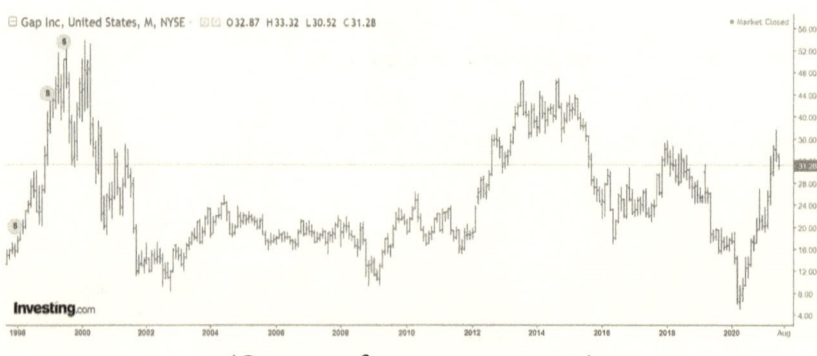

(Courtesy of www.investing.com)

Levi Strauss Monthly Price Chart

(Courtesy of www.investing.com)

## Summarization

Where milk and cotton seed oil cake are linked, I mentioned it at the beginning of this cotton chapter.

And as cotton prices are higher due to various reasons from production/demand issues to weather vagaries, the stocks will fall as companies have to buy cotton at higher prices for their final cloth and brand affecting their earnings for a few quarters and reverse also true.

Here too, just like the other softs, one can make money from both the commodity as well as the stock taking positions simultaneously in opposite directions.

# Chapter 21

## The Future Is Present

### Digitization of Systems

For beginners, it may be difficult to differentiate between digital currency and cryptocurrency (cryptos).

A cryptocurrency is a form of digital asset based on a network that is distributed across a large number of computers. This decentralized structure allows them to exist outside the control of governments and central authorities. It is created with the help of advanced block chain technology to maintain smooth transaction flow.

Digital currency is the electronic model of currency notes and coins that can be stored in the digital wallet. The digital currency can be transformed into cash in hand, if necessary by withdrawing cash from any ATM or bank. It is intangible cash with an open-source contactless transaction flow between two parties. It is a virtual form of fiat currency used in the country.

The cryptocurrency market is broadening itself to become not only a competing asset class versus the gold/bonds but also an alternative asset class for trading and investment.

Since forty years of secular decline in interest rates, this asset class has added zing to returns on investment ratio with quantitative easing and other policies fixed asset classes having already done their hard work.

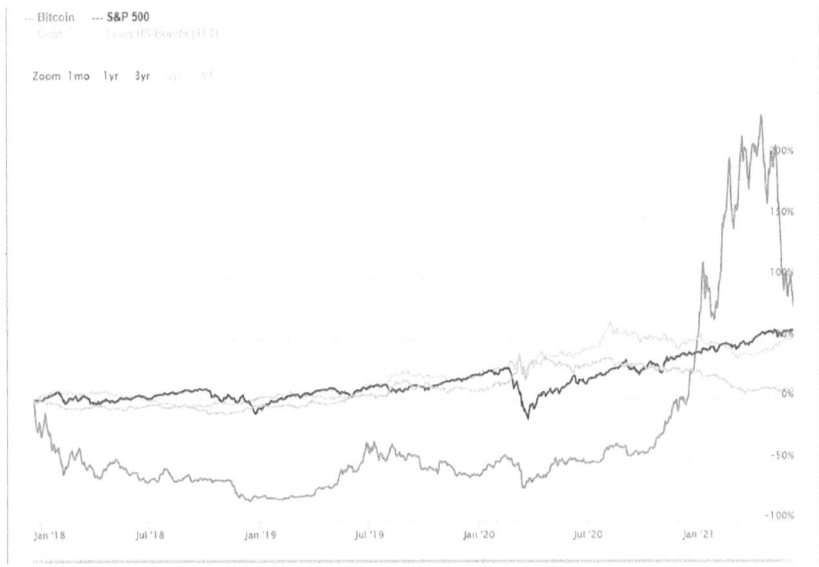

(Courtesy of www.casebitcoin.com)

This class was mainly controlled and traded by the institutions and retail traders and the main Wall Street had no share of the sweet pie.

The shifts in cryptocurrency rates can be credited to the economic law of demand and supply changes. The factors that affected were cross influences of different cryptocurrencies. The widespread acceptance of cryptocurrency has caused the devaluation of national currencies, hence causing the rise in this asset class. Or it can also be said that *Emergence of Cryptos* is a result of the debasement of fiat currencies value due to unabated printing of the paper money.

Positive or negative evaluations have caused wild price movements in the crypto world, especially if these assessments were made by political and economic authorities, either individuals or governments. Various trademark integrations were done and unfolding of political events caused the extreme price changes in the span of last five years. Right from outright banning, introduction of legislations for taxation, categorization as an asset class, introduction of futures contracts, formation of research desk by financial and banking institutions, and the very latest of declaring it as an official legal tender for payment by a country (example, El Salvador).

Currently, the bond yields are extremely low, and in most parts of the world, they are officially negative. So in this context, people have to find an investment avenue that gives them superior returns than the bonds.

A paradigm shift is now happening where institutions are holding cryptos along with gold in their portfolios. As diversification is also happening in balance sheets of countries with some portion of the cash reserves is being diverted into cryptos. So this can result in cash reserves going up and down more than the comfort zone if not managed well.

Increased volatility is the main stay in the modern economy.

Just as one views gold and bonds from five, ten, and thirty years horizons, the same goes with cryptos too. In future massive eruptions and disruptions in cryptos will be witnessed as it starts getting adopted in the mainstream of asset classes by the world. This is going to be most *free & true* form of asset class, eventually becoming a store of value as has been the case till now with precious metals, bonds, real estate, stocks, and any other asset classes.

# Gold and Bitcoin (BTC) Comparative Analysis

| PARAMETERS | GOLD | BITCOIN |
|---|---|---|
| **Store of Value** | Gold has proven to be a store of value especially in uncertain economic times. | BTC is well on its way to become that store of value. |
| **Durability** | Gold is hard to damage or destroy and is corrosion-free. | BTC is digital. so question of damage or corrosion is not possible. Bitcoin is now so mainstream that shutting it down is like pulling the plug to world Internet. |
| **Mining** | Gold is complicated to mine requiring a lot of time, licensing, and expert know-how. | BTC is easier to mine but needs specialized hardware to commence its operations. |
| **Inflation front** | Gold has a stable inflatioNARY adjustment every year, also determining its leased rate over various time horizons. | BTC too gives passive income when *Staked* (currently being 3% PA). |
| **Scarcity** | Gold has no limitations on supply front. There is a lot of gold in ground as well as in oceans. | Maximum supply of BTC is limited to twenty-one million as the design of the program, and that is a certainty. |
| **Divisibility** | Gold is indivisible. One has to do with gold coins and again not convenient to | One BTC is divisible into one hundred million pieces, called Satoshis, and the parts can be |
|  | work with adjusting its weightage to value easily. | used to pay for tangible purchases. |
| **5-year returns** | 5,900% | 48% |
| **Portability** | Portability of gold is possible only to a limited extent. | BTC can be moved in a wallet—online and offline. |

## Investment Case

At current prices of $1,900 per ounce, gold has market capital-ization of $10 trillion.

At $50,000, BTC has a market cap of $1 trillion.

Since 1971, from the Bretton Woods Agreement, gold is up 5000 percent. It was $35 per ounce then.

Whereas since 2010 inception, BTC is up 5,460,000 percent from $1 to $50,000.

In comparison, gold is up 70 percent since 2010.

BTC has outperformed gold on 99 percent of all days.

A very interesting case of statistics is on the Internet, and since the source is unavailable, the credit is absent, but the work presented speaks volumes.

## Investment Case Trend and Facts

| FUTURE CASE PREFERENCE | BITCOIN | GOLD |
|---|---|---|
| Younger generation preference | 1 | 0 |
| Digitization of everything | 1 | 0 |
| Decentralization of everything | 1 | 0 |
| Broken money system | 1 | 1 |
| Uncertain economic times | 1 | 1 |
| Hedge against inflation | 1 | 1 |
| Big money and institutions | 1 | 1 |
| Investment potential | 1 | 0 |
| Investment record last decade | 1 | 0 |
| Volatility and proven record | 0 | 1 |
| Further development potential | 1 | 0 |
| Total | 10 | 5 |

# The Prelude

This is coming out as a penultimate chapter exactly opposite to its meaning because here I want to introduce the three economical pillars on which I base all my analytical cycles of all asset classes.

**Dynamic Disequilibrium**

The cycles are shorter in nature, and volatility is heavy as the asset gets affected due to all kinds of news and FUD. They could be weather related, policy changes, or sudden substitution effect. This is the place where people with lesser capital can speculate for convincing swings in the market that can be read into.

**Static Disequilibrium**

Here the cycles of the assets are more stable and seasonal in nature repeating themselves over a certain time zone again and again. These cycle one sees mostly in agriculture-related commodities and stocks, like sugar where the crop cycle is long, and so is its movement in either direction for itself as well as for the stocks.

**Dynamic Equilibrium**

This is a stage where a speculator's patience is tested. Here, the cycle of the asset becomes very stable and range bound and is to be seen as calmness before the storm. It would be at a major turning point, and one needs to go through all the parameters brought in this book to know what is likely to happen next...

# The Progressive Future

Huge money is to be made in the upcoming stocks connected to the following:

- Space travel
- 3D print technology
- Robotics
- Genome sequencing

And all of them will have many commodities on which they will depend on...

Until we meet again!

# About the Author

Kushal Thaker, the Specunomist, has been in the markets for twenty-five years and now is bringing the vast experience and insight of the markets in this first book.

He has been a consultant to many institutions, corporates, and high net worth, wealthy individuals. His workshops and speeches on various forums across the globe have led to identifying money-making opportunities for the attendees and delegates in the simplest manner.

He is a proponent of "still more, never enough."

www.ingramcontent.com/pod-product-compliance
Lightning Source LLC
Chambersburg PA
CBHW021416210526
45463CB00001B/400